WARRIOR • 132

US ARMY LONG-RANGE PATROL SCOUT IN VIETNAM 1965–71

GORDON L ROTTMAN   ILLUSTRATED BY ADAM HOOK

First published in Great Britain in 2008 by Osprey Publishing,
Midland House, West Way, Botley, Oxford OX2 0PH, UK
43-01 21st Street, Suite 220B, Long Island City, NY 11101, USA
Email: info@ospreypublishing.com

Osprey Publishing is part of the Osprey Group.

Transferred to digital print on demand 2014.

First published 2008
2nd impression 2014

Printed and bound by PrintOnDemand-Worldwide.com,
Peterborough, UK.

A CIP catalogue record for this book is available from the
British Library.

ISBN: 978 1 84603 250 9

Page layout by Mark Holt
Index by Sandra Shotter
Typeset in Sabon and Myriad Pro
Maps from author's own collection
Originated by PPS Grasmere Ltd, Leeds, UK

The Woodland Trust

Osprey Publishing are supporting the Woodland Trust, the UK's
leading woodland conservation charity, by funding the
dedication of trees.

www.ospreypublishing.com

Artist's note

Readers may care to note that the original paintings from which
the color plates in this book were prepared are available for
private sale. The Publishers retain all reproduction copyright
whatsoever. All inquiries should be addressed to:

Scorpio Gallery, 158 Mill Road, Hailsham, East Sussex
BN27 2SH, UK
Email: scorpiopaintings@btinternet.com

The Publishers regret that they can enter into no
correspondence upon this matter.

Acknowledgments

The author is indebted to Shelby Stanton, Stéphane Moutin-
Luyet, Trey Moore of Moore Militaria, Mindy Rosewitz of the US
Army Communications-Electronics Museum, and Steve
Sherman of RADIX Press for their assistance.

Abbreviations

AIT	Advanced Individual Training
AO	Area of Operations
ARVN	Army of the Republic of Vietnam
BCT	Basic Combat Training
C&C	Command and Control
CO	Commanding Officer
IAD	Immediate Action Drills
LRP	Long-Range Patrol
LRRP	Long-Range Reconnaissance Patrol
LZ	Landing Zone
MACV	Military Assistance Command, Vietnam
MOS	Military Occupation Specialty
NATO	North Atlantic Treaty Organization
NCO	Non-Commissioned Officer
NVA	North Vietnamese Army
O&I	Operations & Intelligence
PZ	Pick-up Zone
RON	Remain Overnight
SAS	Special Air Service
SF	Special Forces
SOI	Signal Operating Instructions
SOP	Standard Operating Procedures
TAOR	Tactical Area of Responsibility
TL	Team Leader
TO&E	Table of Organization and Equipment
USARV	US Army, Vietnam
VC	Viet Cong
WP	White Phosphorous ("Willie Pete")
XO	Executive Officer (second-in-command)

CONTENTS

US ARMY LONG-RANGE PATROL SCOUT IN VIETNAM 1965-72

INTRODUCTION

When US Army conventional infantry units began to arrive in the Republic of Vietnam (RVN, or South Vietnam) in May 1965 they found a country of rugged mountains and hills, open plains, dense forests, and vast delta marshes and swamps. The climate was hot, humid, and dry – or hot, humid, and wet. Yet the terrain and unpleasant climate were not the only difficulties that awaited the units. The local Viet Cong (VC) guerrillas and the North Vietnamese Army (NVA) regulars opposing them were highly mobile, traveled light and fast, and were not burdened with a significant logistics tail as the Americans were. Indeed, the enemy was elusive, blended into the population, and could chose when and where to strike. The US-allied forces reacted. They reacted with massed artillery, fighter-bombers, helicopter gunships, and infantry transported in by helicopters. But the enemy often managed to fade into the countryside. Their own logistics bases were across the border in Cambodia and Laos, close but essentially unreachable due to diplomatic considerations.

It became increasingly obvious that this was a war for which the US Army was not prepared. The Army was organized, trained, and equipped to fight a conventional war in Europe or Korea. It was prepared for high-tempo mobile operations involving massed armor and artillery; nuclear, chemical, and biological warfare; electronic warfare; and massive use of airpower against a larger enemy force with similar capabilities. Army doctrine focused on seizing and retaining terrain. An operation order directed a unit to occupy a hill. If the enemy was on the hill or was encountered en route, he was destroyed. If the hill was unoccupied by the enemy, the unit secured it and prepared to fight off attackers or to continue their mission.

Vietnam proved to be an entirely different kind of war. Seizing and holding terrain seldom accomplished much: the enemy had no need to seize and hold terrain. It wanted to seize and control the population. To destroy the enemy, the enemy had to be found – found while he was moving to attack US-allied forces, exploiting the civilian population, or withdrawing after doing so. The enemy's scattered base areas, weapons caches, infiltration trails, and troop concentrations also had to be found to keep him off balance. Once the enemy was located he could then be engaged with overwhelming firepower, and air mobility ensured that troops could be rapidly deployed at any time and from unexpected directions. But first the enemy had to be found.

This proved to be a much more difficult task than imagined. Traditional reconnaissance and surveillance assets, including fixed and rotary-wing aircraft, satellite surveillance, radio intercept and direction finding, ground surveillance radar, armored cavalry units, and other conventional means were of only limited value. The Army soon began reverting to less conventional means to locate the enemy. Acoustic motion sensors were dropped from aircraft and monitored, scout and tracker dog teams were utilized, defecting enemy soldiers were employed as scouts and guides, and a "people-sniffer" was even developed to detect human scents from helicopters.

In dense terrain where the enemy could easily hide, scouts could also move about comparatively undetected. It was found that "putting eyes on the

A Long Range Patrol (LRP) team of the 173rd Airborne Brigade stands by to load aboard a Huey for insertion, early 1967. Different styles of wear of their boonie hats is apparent. (Photo by Co Rentmeester/Time Life Pictures/Getty Images)

Helicopters were used extensively to insert LRP units into the field. Here troopers prepare an 80ft aluminium rung extraction ladder to rig it into a Huey. The rope woven through the center of the rungs is used to pull the ladder back up. (US Army)

5

ground" in the form of small reconnaissance teams, using extreme caution to avoid detection, sometimes achieved success in locating the enemy. US General Westmoreland realized the need for Long Range Patrol (LRP) units soon after taking over Military Assistance Command, Vietnam (MACV) in June 1964, although their formation was not officially approved for another two years.

The concept of and the doctrine for such units already existed, but it was intended for operations behind enemy lines on a conventional European linear-front battlefield. However, units were not available for deployment to Vietnam, and instead they had to be created. The situation in Vietnam called for dedicated specialized infantry units that were organized, trained, and equipped to conduct intelligence collection and surveillance in small teams within enemy-controlled territory.

LRP units

First, an understanding of the designation of these units is necessary. From the early 1960s they were called long-range reconnaissance patrol (LRRP) units. In the mid-1960s they were commonly known as long-range patrol (LRP). "Reconnaissance" was dropped because the units were sometimes assigned other missions and, according to some, as a way of simplifying the designation. Through the 1960s the terms LRP and LRRP were used interchangeably, and both were even used in the same official reports. Both terms are pronounced "Lurp." It is incorrect, however, to use the word "Lurp" in text to identify these units (even though it is written that way in some books). Officially, they were identified as an Infantry Airborne Company (Long-Range Patrol). On January 1, 1969, they were redesignated an Infantry Airborne Company (Ranger), but their mission did not change. No Ranger units had existed since 1951, and the redesignation as Ranger was simply to restore a traditional title. In World War II and the Korean War, Ranger units were primarily raider or strike units. LRP units, while they might undertake occasional small-scale direct-action missions, were chiefly passive reconnaissance units and not "commandos."

The earliest US Army unit that could be considered LRP was the Alamo Scouts, who served in the Southwest Pacific in World War II.[1] They mainly conducted passive reconnaissance missions, operated in six-man teams, and used a peer evaluation system in training that was later adopted by the Ranger Course. In 1961 two provisional LRP companies were formed in West Germany to support V and VII US Corps. These units were formalized in 1965, being assigned a table of organization and equipment (TO&E).

US military histories seldom mention that US LRP doctrine is an offspring of the LRP concept developed by NATO in 1960. Largely based on British Special Air Service concepts of deploying small patrols behind enemy lines, units reported enemy movements and rear area targets via long-range radios. The patrols would be inserted by foot, helicopter, or parachute, or left as stay-behind elements as the Soviets advanced into Germany. They also provided targeting for air and missile strikes on Soviet follow-on echelons. Each NATO country formed LRP units of one or more companies, and battalions in some cases. The operational concept of most of these units was to dig completely concealed hides overlooking main avenues of approach. They reported intelligence using single-sideband radios transmitting in Morse code to rear area base stations. For the most part these units were under corps control, as were the early US units.

1 See Osprey BTO 12, *US Special Warfare Units in the Pacific Theater 1941–45.*

However, the Americans never fully embraced the hide concept and preferred more active patrolling – perhaps because the US military tends not to have the necessary patience for such techniques and prefers to be more proactive.

The existence of the two-corps LRP companies and a couple of provisional platoon-sized units within the US Army prior to Vietnam was not widely known. They trained hard, participating in major exercises, exchanged lessons learned with NATO LRPs, and pioneered operational techniques. The volunteers for these early LRP units were paratroopers with service in the 82nd and 101st Airborne Divisions. Some had served in Special Forces (SF) and would return to the Green Berets while others later volunteered for SF. These LRPs often undertook the Ranger Course or the Pathfinder Course, as well as training with NATO LRRP units. Many of these soldiers wound up in LRP units in Vietnam and were invaluable, passing on their skills to the new units being raised to operate in the jungles and rice paddies of Southeast Asia.

This book is confined to the experience of soldiers within LRP units, specifically airborne LRP units. The experiences of nonairborne LRPs were identical except that they did not attend jump school. The specifics of Vietnam-era recruiting, basic and infantry training, pay, barracks life, and other aspects of nonairborne troops can be found in Osprey Warrior 98, *US Army Infantryman in Vietnam 1965–73*.

CHRONOLOGY

1945
July 21   Vietnam divided at the 17th Parallel as the French forces are withdrawn from Indo-China.

1955
March   First US military advisors arrive in Vietnam.

Many LRPs and Rangers volunteered to escape from line companies with their more regimented way of life. (US Army)

1959

January	North Vietnam issues resolution that changes its "political struggle" in South Vietnam to an "armed struggle."
June	North Vietnam begins developing the Ho Chi Minh Trail to the Republic of Vietnam (RVN), the official name of South Vietnam.

1960

December	National Liberation Front (Viet Cong, or VC) is formed.

1961

July 15	First two US LRP companies are formed in Germany.

1964

August 2–4	Destroyers USS *Maddox* and *C. Turner Joy* allegedly attacked by North Vietnamese torpedo boats in the Gulf of Tonkin.
August 7	US Congress passes Gulf of Tonkin Resolution to counter North Vietnamese aggression.

1965

February 7	VC attack US installations in Pleiku. President Johnson authorizes air attacks on North Vietnam, which commence on February 24.
March 8	First US Marine ground combat troops arrive in the RVN.
April 6	US ground troops authorized to conduct offensive operations.
May 7	First US Army conventional ground combat troops arrive in the RVN.
December	First provisional LRRP unit formed in Vietnam (1st Bde, 101st Abn Div LRRP Platoon).

1966

July 8	General Westmoreland issues directive authorizing provisional LRP units.
August	Projects OMEGA and SIGMA established by Special Forces (SF) to provide LRP support to Army commands.
September 15	Military Assistance Command, Vietnam (MACV) Recondo School established to train LRPs and other US-allied reconnaissance troops.

1967

November 1	Projects OMEGA and SIGMA absorbed into MACV-SOG.
December 20	All provisional LRP units become approved units and are assigned formal unit designations.

1968

January 30	VC and North Vietnamese Army (NVA) initiate Tet Offensive, which ends on February 26, 1968.
March 31	US government announces deescalation of its war effort and halts bombing of North Vietnam.
May 12	Peace talks begin in Paris.

1969

February 1	All LRP units reflagged as Ranger companies of the 75th Infantry.

1970

December 19	MACV Recondo School closed.

1972

July 16	Last LRP mission conducted in Vietnam (Team 72, H-75).
August 15	Last Ranger company (H-75) in Vietnam stands down.

1973

January 15	US government announces the cessation of all offensive ground action.
January 27	Cease-fire agreement is signed in Paris; US conscription ceases.
March 29	Final US troops withdrawn from RVN; MACV is disbanded.

RECRUITMENT

There was no central controlling headquarters or organization managing LRP/Ranger units and their personnel. Each was an independent unit under the direct control of its parent command. The recruiting and training of personnel, as well as standards, varied between units.

Most men volunteering as LRPs were three-year volunteers. They were regular army enlisted men with any number of reasons for signing up during an unpopular war: a desire for adventure, patriotism, idealism, an interest in a military career, a need for a job, or to leave a bad home situation. Draftees serving for two years also volunteered. Many African-Americans and Hispanics volunteered for the airborne, either because it was more of a challenge, with the opportunity to prove themselves, or simply for the extra money to send home thanks to the jump pay. However, smaller numbers of minorities served in LRPs, although the reasons are not entirely clear.

While LRP/Ranger units were considered "airborne," in many cases they were nonairborne-qualified. The troops were originally recruited from infantry battalions within their parent division/brigades. Even in airborne divisions and brigades some assigned troops were nonairborne. While airborne qualification was desirable, mainly because of the inherent esprit de corps, self-confidence, and physical fitness that were a result of airborne training, it was not essential. Indeed, no LRP team was ever inserted by parachute. Only the companies assigned to the 173nd Airborne Brigade (75th Det/N-75), 101st Airborne Division (F-58/L-75), and the two fields forces (E-20/C-75, F-51/D-75, D-151) were maintained close to fully airborne-qualified.

Overall, recruiting was an ongoing struggle. LRPs demanded highly qualified soldiers, and infantry battalions were reluctant to relinquish their best men. A divisional LRP company required some 100 potential fire team and squad leaders at a time when infantry battalions already suffered from a lack of qualified leaders. Some men in line units volunteered for a change: to get out of a unit they did not like, for the challenge, to be part of an elite unit, or to serve with professionals rather than alongside possibly less enthusiastic line company troops. All volunteers had to convince their commanders to let them transfer. LRP NCOs did recruit from the division/brigade replacement training center, but such individuals had only four months of basic and infantry training; their lack of in-country experience was a deficit. Men with several months' experience in line units were preferred, but such volunteers may have had only six months remaining in their tour, and they still had to be trained and gain further experience on patrols. Line company volunteers were sought to attend the MACV Recondo School, but in all probability those showing promise would be assigned to the LRP unit upon completion. LRP officers were more experienced, having already served as rifle platoon commanders and were often Ranger-qualified, while company commanders were usually on their second tour.

The criteria sought for a LRP varied between units, but generally included someone between the ages of 20 and 21 (as they were more mature and had greater stamina than 18–19-year-olds), a high school education or a 100 GT score,[2] a clean police record, and a high degree of physical fitness. Other desirable traits might include rural, hunting, or outdoor experience, or an athletic background. LRPs also required less tangible qualities such as patience, self-control, self-confidence, psychological stability, and the willingness to work as a member of a close-knit team.

Volunteers were interviewed by the company commander or a panel of officers and NCOs in an effort to appraise their suitability. Just as important, they were told what was in store for them, the danger of their missions, and the high standards expected of them. As a result, volunteers were fully aware that they would be required to infiltrate enemy-controlled areas in four- to eight-man teams, avoiding contact and with extraction a dangerously long time coming.

In order to attract qualified personnel and recognize their efforts, units implemented different benefits and privileges that included:
- Distinctive insignia such as company scrolls or pocket patches
- Distinctive headgear such as berets or authorization to wear boonie hats in base camp
- Priority consideration for promotion when eligible
- Special attention to awards
- A minimum of a 36-hour standdown between missions
- Additional out-of-country (seven-day) or in-country (three-day) R&R (normally only one of each granted)
- Frequent articles on the unit in division/brigade newsletters

2 General Technical skill test, a type of IQ test. An infantryman required at least a 70, Special Forces 100, and Officer Candidate School 110.

TRAINING

There was no formal LRP training course. The optimistic prewar training scheme for a LRP company required eight months of intensive unit and individual training. It unrealistically included all leaders and recon team personnel attending the eight-week Ranger Course as well as the three-week Pathfinder Course. However, training slots for those courses were simply not available. Most units were raised in-country from men with previous LRP experience, sometimes transferred from existing units in Vietnam – Special Forces and Ranger-qualified NCOs, and inexperienced volunteers. Only three companies (E-50, F-58, D-151) were trained first in the States.

LRPs were for the most part infantrymen; specifically, light weapons infantrymen with Military Occupation Specialty (MOS) 11B.[3] This meant they had eight weeks of Basic Combat Training (BCT) and eight weeks of Light Weapons Infantryman Advanced Individual Training (AIT). Many, but not all, infantry volunteering for parachute training upon enlistment undertook AIT at Fort Gordon, GA, the Army's only "airborne-oriented" infantry training center. It was little different from AIT at any of the other six infantry training centers. But trainees were armed with M16 rifles while other training centers still had M14s, they sang a lot of airborne Jody calls during runs, and their physical training was more oriented to passing the Airborne physical fitness test. Besides 11Bs, other infantrymen who served as LRPs included mortar men (11C), antitank gunners (11H), and cavalry scouts (11D).

Regardless of the degree of training and experience of a LRP volunteer, few had previously served in LRP units. Ranger training, while focusing on patrolling and leadership skills, did not provide the very specialized training necessary for LRPs. Each LRP unit had its own methods of operation and specific types of missions, and operated on different terrain against a variable enemy.

Airborne students wait their turn on training apparatuses while they observe other students to learn from their mistakes. Here a Black Hat has just ordered, "Hit it!" and the students immediately jump up, assume the exit position and count to six thousand. It was a ploy to keep students on their toes and from dozing off. The Black Hat wears a black windbreaker adorned with Ranger and Airborne tabs over the Infantry School patch. (US Army)

Units were responsible for training their own replacements. At times the personnel loss rate was so high with men rotating home that units had to stand down to recruit and train. LRP unit courses lasted from one to two weeks, working eight to twelve hours a day, with the course run by experienced patrol members. No two courses were alike, even within the same unit, as they were constantly modified with lessons learned. Training was normally a brief lecture and demonstration followed by hands-on exercises. The range of subjects was broad and included physical conditioning, marksmanship, enemy

---

3 A complete MOS code included a skill level (1 = PVT, PFC; 2 = SP4; 4 = SGT, SSG, SFC, MSG, 1SG; 5 = SGM). "3" was for noninfantry SP4s with more technical skills. A special skill identifier was appended (P = Parachutist, G = Ranger, 0 = no special skill). A parachute-qualified SP4 would be an 11B2P while a Ranger-qualified SSG would be an 11B4G ("P" would not be included even if he was parachute qualified).

weapons familiarization, load packing, camouflage, noise and light discipline, movement techniques, immediate action drills (IAD), helicopter loading and off-loading, land navigation, hand signals, radio procedures, calling for artillery and medical evacuation (medevac), directing helicopter gunships, emergency treatment of wounds, patrolling techniques, helicopter rappelling, and extraction techniques. Units conducting direct-action missions would include demolitions, machine gun familiarization, and ambush training.

Most courses were concluded by the conduct of at least an overnight security patrol or an ambush patrol outside the base camp. No more than two "newbies" were assigned to a team, and their training and evaluation continued under the supervision of experienced LRPs. It could require up to three months of frequent patrols for a man to become fully qualified.

A student vigorously exits the 34ft tower. He will fall only a few feet before sliding down the cables to the mound. The sensation is not unlike, in some aspects, jumping from an aircraft in flight. (US Army)

Jump school

Airborne qualification proved a soldier was highly motivated, physically fit, and could control his apprehension. Predeployment combat training, no matter how realistic, is still moderated by safety constraints. Participants know that it is training, and while accidents happen, they are comparatively rare. Battlefield sights and sounds can be partly replicated, as can stress and exhaustion through constant action, demanding tasks, sleep and food deprivation, and poor weather. Yet it is still training, and the fear and stress of combat cannot be replicated to anywhere near the intensity of the real thing.

It is a different matter for one to strap on a heavy load of equipment and board a hot or freezing aircraft for a bouncing, noisy ride with airsick fellow passengers and feel the tension build as it roars toward the drop zone (DZ). The paratroopers hurl themselves from an aircraft with complete trust that the parachute will open, knowing they face any number of landing hazards and the possibility of injury. The tension felt by paratroopers about to exit during a training jump is little different from that experienced when inbound to a hot landing zone (LZ). The difference is that the paratroopers have learned to manage their fear and deal with stress.

The Airborne Course was three weeks of highly focused, physically demanding instruction. The appeal for volunteers was the esprit de corps, assignment to a quality unit, the paratrooper's trappings, and the addition of jump pay. Many LRPs had undertaken airborne training. It was a critical assessment of whether a soldier was suitable for specialist training. Even if LRPs were never inserted by air, their airborne training was a hugely important part of their predeployment training.

Airborne volunteers were assigned to the 4th Student Battalion, The Student Brigade, Infantry School, Fort Benning, GA. The battalion's 41st–49th Companies typically numbered 300–500 students, of which 15–30 were officers. At the time, regular army combat arms officers were also required to attend either jump school or the Ranger Course. There might be a few men from other services attending the course alongside these potential LRP Scouts.

Flying into Atlanta, GA, or bussed from AIT centers, the aspirant paratroopers reported in and were assigned to a training company. Two companies, for example the 45th and 49th, were paired for a class with 600–900 students including recycles from the previous class. Within a company, students were assigned in alphabetical order and given a "chalk number," which was stenciled on their helmet. Companies were then divided into three platoons of four "sticks."

The class assembled during Zero Week and was given the airborne PT test. The class was required to pass the Army Physical Fitness Test for the 17–21 age group (one-mile run, sit-ups, push-ups, chin-ups, horizontal ladder, grenade throw, low-crawl, and a run, dodge and jump). They also met their platoon's TAC NCO (Tactical Advisor and Counselor – pronounced "tac"). The TACs were not instructors, but they were responsible for the men in the company area and for getting them to and from the training area.

At 0500hrs on a Monday morning the students were roused for reveille to start on their road to becoming a paratrooper. Their uniform was simply fatigues, combat boots, and a steel helmet. The uniforms had to be starched and boots spit-shined. Breakfast was rushed: food was aplenty, but only six minutes were allotted to eating it. The companies double-timed to the training area to begin Ground Week. Filing into bleachers they were greeted by Colonel "Bill" Welch, the Airborne Department's director though much of the war. Welch told the aspirants they had one goal: to learn how to safely parachute from an aircraft. Standing in the background were the Black Hats, the instructors identifiable by their black baseball caps.

The Black Hats ran the trainees through inspection, dropping students for push-ups for each infraction. Black Hats were referred to as "Sergeant," and student officers were given normal courtesies, but there was no requirement to salute them on the training grounds. The Black Hats addressed officers as "Sir" but treated them no differently than other students, dropping them for push-ups just as readily as a private – "Give me ten, Sir." If wearing a parachute harness, ten squat jumps were given. On the training grounds, if a student took more than one step he ran. If he took only one step he hopped. When still, he stood at parade rest. There was a ten-minute break every hour, but the students ran to and from the break area, and the transit time was included in the "break." After inspection, platoons hit the gravel track for a two-mile run, singing airborne Jody calls – ritualistic chants disparaging the useless "legs," or nonjumpers, and the valor and esteem of paratroopers. This was done in formation and in step, making for a grueling run compared to running at one's own pace. If a student fell out he had to keep moving and still finish the run. To stop was to quit. The sticks double-timed to their training stations, rotating hourly in a modified "country fair" system. That is, the Black Hat led each stick to the next station and taught the class himself rather than using a dedicated instructor. Instruction began with a lecture and demonstration. Everything else was performance-oriented: doing it repeatedly until it became automatic. During Ground Week the trainees learned the nine jump commands, door exit procedures, and what they had to do during Jumpmaster inspection, as well as mastering the parachute landing fall (PLF). This was done without equipment, and then with a harness and dummy reserve. Sticks were taught to roll with the direction of the wind drift, distributing the impact of the fall along the "five points of contact" with the feet and knees together, arms up protecting the head, fists balled, and elbows tucked in: 1) balls of the feet, 2) calf, 3) thigh,

4) buttocks,[4] and 5) side of the back. This was repeated over and over off a 2ft platform into a sawdust pit until the PLF became second nature. The Black Hats constantly corrected, guided, and gave hints to performing better techniques. They had the students' best interest at heart and inspired them through their dedicated professionalism and attention to details. Internal contusions, scrapes, strains, and pulled muscles were common, with students loading themselves down with aspirin, elastic bandages, and muscle ointments from the PX rather than reporting for sick call and risk missing so much training that they had to be recycled.

A couple of days into training all eyes were on the first stick to climb the 34ft (10.4m) tower. This tower replicated C-130 transport troop doors. On each side of the compartment were four cables running at a downward angle 150ft (45m) to a 10ft (3m) earth berm, called "the mound." The cables were anchored to poles behind the mound. Cables stretched between the poles stopped the jumper before he reached them. On each cable was a trolley wheel to which were attached 8ft (2.4m) straps with shock absorbers. Outfitted in a parachute harness with a dummy reserve, the stick double-timed up the four flights of stairs after being Jumpmaster-checked. Two Black Hats inside fastened the harness' web risers to the trolley straps. Abbreviated jump commands were given, and the student assumed the exit position. On the command "GO!" the trainee performed a hard exit as it was essential that the jumper completely clear the aircraft. Pushing hard with his arms and springing with his legs, the jumper hurled out the door, legs stiff, elbows tucked hard against his sides, hands gripping the reserve, and chin down, while counting out loud from one thousand to six thousand. (During an actual jump, if the paratrooper did not feel the opening shock by that time, he pulled his reserve.) As his short fall came to the end of the trolley straps, he felt the jerk that simulated his canopy opening, and he slid down the cable to the mound. There, students below each of the cables – called "mound men" – waited to grab the jumper and unhook him. The jumper then double-timed back to the tower, and the Black Hat critiqued him from the door. Another student, on the ground below the mound – the "rope man" – snapped a rope to the trolley straps and ran back to the tower where the Black Hat grabbed the straps and unclipped the rope. Students awaiting their turn sat in bleachers watching each jumper and listening to critiques. The 34ft tower was the great separator. Anyone refusing to jump or unable to master the procedures was gone. During the week a student made over a dozen 34ft-tower jumps. With Ground Week completed, the weekend offered no rest, but rather long days on KP, polishing boots, and getting uniforms ready for Tower Week.

The second week proved to be even more demanding, physically and technically. Two-mile runs and PT began each morning. There were more PLFs and 34ft-tower jumps with four men rapidly exiting each door, simulating a "mass jump." Being dragged by a parachute in high winds was serious, and recovery methods were taught using wind machines to drag students behind an inflated canopy. In lower winds they were taught to roll onto their feet and outrun the canopy, turning into the wind and collapsing the canopy. In higher winds when it was impossible to regain one's feet, the canopy quick-releases

A student jumper makes a parachute landing fall (PLF) on Lee Drop Zone, Alabama. His feet should be together. Feet spread apart could result in one foot taking more impact than the other, possibly causing a sprain if not a break. (US Army)

4 Leading to the phrase, "He has his head up his fourth point of contact."

The student's view from the 34ft-tower door, looking toward the mound with detail students standing ready to receive "trolley troopers" sliding down the cables. Four sets of cables run from each side of the tower to the anchoring poles. (US Army)

("Capewells") on the harness were released and the canopy collapsed. The least popular training device was the "suspended harness." The "nutcracker," or "suspended agony," saw the student strapped into a harness alongside a platform. He practiced slips and turns by pulling on the risers to "steer" the canopy. Not much more popular was the "swing landing trainer" described in Plate A. Trainees learned in-aircraft procedures and more about the 35ft (10.7m) diameter T-10 parachute. They also learned emergency actions if landing in trees, water, or electrical power lines; the procedures necessary for different types of parachute malfunctions; how to deploy a 24ft (7.3m) diameter reserve parachute; and what to do if the static line failed to separate and they were towed by the aircraft. Tower Week drew its name from the three 250ft (76.2m) towers; usually only one or two drops were made from them. In these jumps, the student was harnessed, and a special canopy was attached to a large ring that was hoisted up and released. He immediately hauled down on his risers to slip away from the tower with the wind, but he had to quickly turn sideways into the wind. The Black Hat shouted bullhorn instructions until the trainee PLFed into the sawdust. After hundreds of push-ups and squat jumps, miles of running, being twisted and turned every which way, and suffering countless aches and pains, the first two weeks were behind the trainees.

Weather and aircraft cooperating, Jump Week was only three days long, with one jump on Monday and two on each of the following two days. The first two jumps would be individual tap-outs. The last three were mass jumps with all jumpers exiting in a pass. The first four jumps were "Hollywood jumps" – without equipment. The last jump was with equipment: a sandbag-filled kit bag simulating a pack under the reserve and a weapons container with a board inside attached to the left side.

On Monday morning refresher classes were presented on in-flight emergencies, malfunctions, and emergency landing procedures. Colonel Welch presented the malfunctions class and gave a pep talk assuring the students they were well trained, their equipment reliable, and that they would perform better than they expected. After lunch they bussed to Lawson Army Airfield. In a hangar they were issued parachutes and "chuted-up" after a briefing on all aspects of the jump. The Jumpmasters gave them a detailed inspection and led them to the transports.[5] The Jumpmasters exuded confidence, although the jumpers were in too much of a daze to hesitate.

After takeoff they flew toward Lee Drop Zone in Alabama. At the ten-minute warning, with the red light beside the door blinking on, the Jumpmasters opened the doors. It was actually pretty easy. The Jumpmasters ran through the jump commands, and the students responded to the actions as they had practiced: "Get ready. Outboard personnel stand up. Inboard personnel stand up. Hook up. Check static lines. Check equipment. Sound off for equipment check. Stand in the door." With that command, the number one man on each side pivoted into the door, passing the static line to the Jumpmaster and gripping the inside of the door frame. As the aircraft roared over the DZ at 1,250ft (381m), the Jumpmaster shouted "GO!" in the jumper's ear and slapped him on the back of the thigh.

When tapped out he pushed hard with his arms and legs rotating toward the aircraft's rear. The falling sensation was brief, only so long as the aircraft's side was in his peripheral vision. As he streaked down shouting, "One thousand! Two thousand!" the 15ft (4.5m) static line stretched behind him, pulling the deployment bag out of his backpack. The 30ft (9.1m) long "S"-folded suspension lines ripped out of their pack tray retaining bands, stretched full-length along with the 3ft (0.9m) web risers connecting them to the harness, and then the 18ft (5.5m) length of folded canopy was pulled from the "D-bag." Everything stretched out to 80ft (24.4m), and the jumper was still attached to the anchor line while the following jumpers were already going out the door. The canopy inflated and the break cord connecting the canopy apex (top) to the static line snapped, releasing his bond to the aircraft. The opening shock, with a properly fitted harness, was surprisingly mild and was absorbed bodywide. This all occurred in four to five seconds. The immediate need was to check for canopy damage and complete opening, and then check for nearby jumpers. Collisions and mutual entanglements were something to be avoided. If a jumper was seen below, the higher man slipped away as the lower canopy robbed air.

One's sensations were overwhelmed with that first experience; the brief fall, the gush of wind and screaming turboprops, bellowing the count and feeling the suspension lines unraveling off one's back, the not uncomfortable bodywide opening tug, the sudden silence, a floating sensation, the horizon-to-horizon vista, the pure exhilaration, and, if one was so fortunate to have turned back toward the rapidly dwindling aircraft, the thrill of seeing bodies hurtling out both doors followed by blossoming canopies.

Regardless of the Black Hats admonishing them to refrain from shouting, there were yells of "Airborne all the way!" Black Hats on the ground shouted instructions to specific jumpers to turn into the wind or to start looking around to avoid another jumper or to prepare to land. The ride was over in less than one minute. The ground rush was coming up fast; a slip to turn sideways, toes down, knees bent, elbows into the sides, and head up looking at the canopy skirt to prevent one from "reaching for the ground" – a reaction that could cause a stiff-legged injury. A thump, bump, and a roll just as he had practiced, and it was over. Then there were heavy tugs on the suspension lines and a quick

5 These may have been Fairchild C-119F Packets ("Flying Boxcar"), Fairchild C-123K
   Providers, or Lockheed C-130H Hercules ("Herc").

scramble to his feet to run around behind the reinflating canopy. The harness was shed and placed into the kit bag. The canopy and suspension lines were figure-eight rolled and stuffed in. Black Hats shouted through bullhorns to double-time off the DZ to the chute turn-in point. As they trotted through the weeds the new paratroopers would meet up and greet one another with shouts of "Airborne!" and "They're paying us for this?"

The next day reality struck. Most paratroopers will confess the hardest jumps they ever made were their second or third, a sort of "What am I doing here?" realization. Nonetheless, the five jumps were completed. After their graduation jump the new paratroopers did not bother to double-time off to the DZ. The students fell into a rather loose formation. Officers worked their way down the ranks shaking each man's hand, handed him his silver wings, and said, "Congratulations, paratrooper." Within a day or two they were on their way to their assignments.

The shirts and trousers of tiger stripes seldom matched in color, pattern, and fabric. Here a distinctive black unit scarf is worn. In the background are helicopter revetments and large aluminum-frame helicopter maintenance shelters without their canvas covers. (John Burford collection)

APPEARANCE

Owing to the heat and humidity, as well as a Spartan diet and strenuous exercise, LRPs for the most part were lean and trim. Looking at period photos of LRPs, one can see a thinner general appearance than a young man of the same age today raised on fast food. Hair styles varied from longish on top, usually cut short on the sides, to very short all around, as it was easier to keep clean and was much cooler. Mustaches were permitted in some units but generally frowned on in the army. "Lifer" NCOs told troops they could grow a mustache if their ID card photo showed them wearing one.

Once assigned to an airborne unit, a paratrooper was authorized to wear his jump wings on a unit-colored oval background on the left breast pocket (over the pocket on field uniforms); the red, white and blue "glider patch" (which also depicted a parachute) on the left front of his garrison cap (officers wore it on the right side – paratroopers did not wear "flying saucer" or "bus driver" service caps); and privately purchased Corcoran jump boots with trousers bloused. The Airborne tab over shoulder patches was worn by all unit personnel including "legs," identifying the unit and not individuals as airborne.

Technically LRP companies were to wear the parent command, division, or brigade patch with an airborne tab. Most LRP/Ranger units wore some form of unofficial scroll on the left shoulder over the parent unit's patch, often influenced by the World War II Ranger battalion scrolls.

A **AIRBORNE TRAINEE, FORT BENNING**

Jump school was strictly regimented, with every effort made to keep students focused solely on how to safely parachute from an aircraft. Here a Black Hat instructor critiques a student executing a parachute landing fall from the swing landing trainer. Under a shed were 10ft platforms on which the harnessed student stood. He swung off and, oscillating back and forth, other students gradually lowered him with a pulley system until the Black Hat signaled his release a few feet above the sawdust. He might unexpectedly fall forward, rearward, or to the side, and instantly had to assume the correct PLF. Training continued regardless of temperature, hot or cold, and through rain or snow. Here the students wear the M1965 field jacket while the instructor wears the wool shirt. In the summer students wore white undershirts and instructors black. Fort Benning summers were so hot that students were hosed down at hourly intervals.

Examples of LRP/Ranger berets. Left to right: black beret worn by F-58 Infantry displaying the 101st Airborne Division's black-and-white Recondo patch; black beret of a Ranger company displaying the 75th Infantry flash; tiger-stripe beret. There was no standardization between units as to beret insignia. A tiger-stripe beret was worn by some early LRP units – not very practical as field wear. (Trey Moore collection)

The Korean War Ranger companies unofficially wore black berets in 1950–51, the first use of this headgear by Ranger units. In 1967 some of the LRP companies began wearing black berets on an unofficial basis. Other companies locally purchased tiger-stripe berets, mainly for wearing on base as they were poor field headgear. With the redesignation as Ranger companies and the assignment of the 75th Infantry lineage, the black beret was adopted by most companies, but some did not begin wearing it until 1971.

On base, LRPs wore standard olive green (OG) jungle fatigues, OG undershirt and shorts, jungle boots, and prescribed headgear. More commonly they wore only the trousers and undershirt or went bare-chested and bare-headed. Most men did not wear undershirts or shorts, especially in the field, as they retained moisture and caused chafing and rashes.

Mission uniforms were a different matter. While there was a degree of latitude in what LRPs wore, it was usually standardized in the unit or at least in accord with team SOPs (standard operating procedures). Rather than allowing too much individual variation, many units realized it was wiser for all team members to wear the same uniform, especially headgear. This allowed individuals' silhouettes to be more readily identified.

The most commonly worn uniform was three-color tiger stripes, which became a symbol of LRPs. These were not official issue but either locally purchased or obtained by special requests through supply channels. Tiger stripes originated in the early 1960s, being introduced by SF advisors to the Civilian Irregular Defense Group (CIDG) and Vietnamese Marine Corps. They were produced in Okinawa, South Korea, and Thailand by many contractors. This resulted in a variety of patterns, colorations, and fabric weights. While identified with elite units and widely popular, there were numerous complaints about the uniform. Being less durable than American uniforms, the fabric and stitching easily ripped, dyes faded, thin plastic buttons were easily pulled loose and broken, and the pockets were too small for necessary items. The sizing was also poor, and it was especially difficult to find American sizes. It was even common for shirts and trousers to be mismatched in color and pattern. Troops would have local tailors cannibalize uniforms to sew in panels to create larger sizes, to sew on US jungle fatigue buttons, to reinforce seams, and to replace pockets with larger ones. No insignia were worn.

After a great deal of study and indecision the Army finally adopted a camouflage uniform for special units in early 1967. Developed by the Engineer Research and Development Laboratory in 1948, the four-color woodlands pattern was applied to jungle fatigues. They did not see wide issue until the end of 1967 and into summer 1968. Known as "camies" they proved to be popular in both color/pattern and wearability, gradually replacing tiger stripes.

However, neither pattern was adequate for the many variations of vegetation throughout Vietnam. There were instances where normal OG jungle fatigues were better. Splotches or bands of black paint were sometimes sprayed on "jungles." While sometimes done by SF recon teams, LRPs very rarely donned black uniforms in an effort to appear as VC from a distance.

Headgear was usually a "boonie hat" or "jungle hat," officially a hot weather or tropical hat, a full-brimmed hat with a flat-topped crown. Issue hats came in various styles but were colored OG and later woodlands camouflage. Tiger-stripe boonie hats were locally purchased and were found in a wide variety of styles, colors, and patterns. Boonie hats were often personalized in indelible ink with names, slogans, and symbols. There was often a great sense of attachment to boonie hats. Headscarves and headbands, usually made from triangular bandages or undershirt cloth, were also sometimes worn. They were discouraged as they presented a piratelike image, but they kept sweat out of the eyes and were not knocked off by vegetation.

Clothing was loose to allow air circulation, but if too loose it would snag on vegetation. Sleeves were worn down for camouflage, and trousers were usually bloused into boots. It was not uncommon to tie "550 cord" (olive drab, or OD, parachute suspension line) or boot laces around the calves to reduce snagging and leech infiltration. Besides issue trouser belts, many men wore a shortened A7A cargo strap ("rigger belt") or a doubled length of $^5/_8$-in. nylon rope tied with a square knot. Sweat cloths or "drive-on rags," were very popular. This could be an OD triangular bandage (36x36x56in.), an issue OG terry cloth towel, or an issue OG tropical combat neckerchief (24x36in.) draped or loosely tied around the neck. They were used to mop sweat and dirt from the face, neck, and hands; to clean weapons and ammunition; to wrap around the handguard of hot weapons; to secure prisoners; and as an emergency tourniquet. In some instances gloves were worn as an aid for busting through brush, especially in areas with thorny plants and vines. These were black leather glove shells without the knit wool inserts and with the finger tips cut off at the first joint – "recon gloves" – to allow easy use of weapons and equipment, and for air circulation. Cream-colored heavy leather work gloves were used for rappelling. In the central highlands and mountains, troops were issued the lightweight knitted shirt made of OG acetate, the "sleeping shirt." The fast-drying, pullover sweater was worn under camies, especially at night. Patrol uniforms were not washed, and some troops even smoked them so that the smell merged with the environment.

Rangers of Company D, 151st Infantry of the Indiana Army National Guard, the only National Guard infantry unit deployed to Vietnam. They wear woodlands camouflage uniforms and olive green boonie hats or sweat bands. Note the CIB on the nearest man's turned-up hat brim. (US Army)

Overall, however, LRPs maintained a more military appearance and bearing than many other troops. They had their rebellious streaks, and there were exceptions of course, but LRPs were volunteers in select units. Too much deviation was discouraged. Most units did not tolerate the display of peace symbols and other signs of protest.

Camouflage sticks were OD metal tubes with a cap on each end and a push-out solid paint stick with loam (very dark green) and light green on either end. Loam was applied to the shiny, high areas of the face (forehead, cheekbones, nose, chin, jawline, ears) and light green was applied to other areas including the neck, while the backs of hands were done in loam. Many LRPs had favored patterns they applied. Camouflage paint was reapplied ("re-camied") in the morning and as necessary. The "men with green faces" became a trademark of LRPs as conventional infantry seldom "camied up."

ID tags were kept quiet by "dog tag silencers," a thin plastic tube that sheathed the beaded chain and clear plastic covers for the tags. There were also stretchable rubber rims that fitted around the edges of tags, or they could be taped together or simply carried separately: one around the neck and the other in a pocket.

This M16A1 rifle-armed LRP has an AN/PRC-25 radio strapped to his aluminum-frame rucksack. An Air Force survival knife is carried on his pistol belt, and M26 frags are attached to his ammo pouches. (US Army)

EQUIPMENT AND WEAPONS

LRPs used the same equipment as was carried by conventional infantrymen, although the gear was tailored for LRP missions according to duration, mission requirements, and terrain. A factor differentiating LRP equipment requirements from conventional infantrymen was that every man had to be self-sufficient in case he was separated from his team. Not all conventional infantrymen carried a map, compass, air-ground marking gear, and smoke grenades, for example. A good deal of ordnance was carried by each man, usually more than their conventional counterparts.

B **INDIVIDUAL EQUIPMENT AND WEAPONS**

This early LRP (1) wears the signature tiger stripes without insignia, M1956 web gear, and an indigenous rucksack as used by the Civilian Irregular Defense Group (CIDG). At the time no comparable US frameless rucksack existed. He is generously equipped with M18 "colored smokes" and M26 "frags." He has a double 5/8in rope around his waist and wears a headband and neckcloth made from triangular bandages. He has taped a second 20-round magazine to his M16A1 rifle's magazine for quick reload.

The insert items are typical of what a LRP would carry in his ruck, on his web gear, and on his person. 2: M18A1 Claymore antipersonnel mine with 100ft electrical firing wire and M57 "clacker" firing device. 3: M16A1 rifle cleaning kit. 4: XM166 white, XM167 green, XM168 red, and XM169 yellow mini smoke grenades. 5: "Pop-up" ground signal flare (removed from its gray packing container and available in white, green, red, and amber parachute flares and star clusters; here M127A1 white star parachute). 6: Pocket-size fluorescent orange/pink marker panels were cut from 20x72in. VS-17 air-ground marker panels. Some men sewed a panel section into the inside of their hat crown and "flashed" it at aircraft as a signal. 7: Halazone water purification tablets, 50 to a bottle, one per quart. 8: Insect repellent, "bug juice." 9: Foot powder. 10: Poncho liner. 11: Sleeping shirt. 12: Cushion sole boot socks. 13: Acetate-covered AO map. 14: Issue notepad and pencil. 15: Lensatic compass. Carried in a pocket or a first aid pouch and secured to the person by a "dummy cord." 16: Camouflage stick. 17: Snap link (aka carabineer). Anything that could be damaged by water was wrapped in plastic.

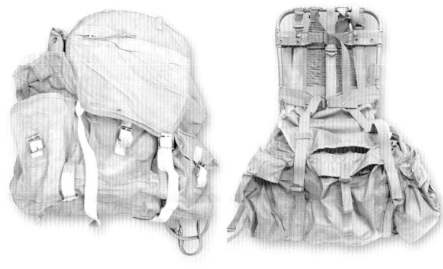

The nylon tropical rucksack was introduced in late 1968. While it allowed equipment to be carried on the belt, its capacity was too small for LRPs, but it was used regardless. (Trey Moore collection)

"Web gear," collectively called "load-bearing equipment" (LBE) or "load-carrying equipment" (LCE), included pistol belts, suspenders, magazine pouches, canteen carriers, first aid pouches, and various special purpose items. Early in the war these were the M1956 made of cotton canvas and webbing. Constant wetting and drying coupled with hard use rapidly wore it out. Cotton gear absorbed up to 40 percent its weight in water, an encumbrance during the monsoon season and when crossing streams. The M1967-modernized LCE began to be issued in 1968, although some units received test versions earlier. This gear was made of nylon, with aluminum and plastic fittings replacing steel and brass hardware. It was lighter, more durable, and absorbed only 8 percent its weight in water. When new it was somewhat shiny and stiff, making a rustling noise in vegetation. It was of basically the same design as the M1956, and it was not uncommon for both types of items to be mixed by individuals. Items such as the small combat packs ("butt pack"), mess kits, entrenching tools, machetes, and bayonets were seldom carried.

A good deal of ammunition was carried, with SOPs typically specifying a minimum of 18–20 20-round M16 magazines (the 30-round was not available). Some men carried more or may have carried a seven-pocket bandolier – with two ten-round stripper clips in each pocket – stowed in the rucksack. One never discarded magazines. Four to six magazine pouches might be carried, with each holding four 20-round magazines. The universal pouches (originally holding two M14 magazines) were too deep for M16 magazines, but troops placed a field dressing in the bottom to raise the magazines. Both shorter M1956-type and M1967 pouches were made for M16 magazines. Magazine pouches were bulky and heavy, and so many men carried two seven-pocket M3 bandoliers with a magazine in each pocket. These cheap cotton bandoliers rapidly wore out, but replacements came in every ammunition can. There were sometimes shortages of magazine pouches, so magazines were loaded in canteen carriers or in an M9 Claymore mine bag.

A major deficiency was the lack of an adequate rucksack. Field gear had been designed for conventional environments with the idea that a soldier would have to carry only one to three C-ration meals at a time. Resupply would be continuous. In Vietnam conventional infantry had to be able to carry at least three days of rations and LRPs often more. The little combat butt pack was totally inadequate. Early on, some units managed to acquire M1951 mountain rucksacks. More commonly used was the lightweight rucksack. This was a nylon combat pack with three external pockets attached to a tubular aluminum frame, usually the bottom portion. A radio could be strapped to the upper frame. The problem with frame rucksacks was that they rode low on the back, preventing items from being attached to pistol belts. Some men wore no web gear, carrying everything attached to the ruck and their magazines in bandoliers. Later a nylon tropical rucksack with three external pockets was issued.

Conventional infantrymen usually shared an inflatable air mattress, poncho, and poncho liner with a buddy. These items increased weight and bulk, but more importantly, they made noise. Air mattresses required a lot of huffing and puffing to inflate and made crinkling noises, as did ponchos. LRPs simply did not use them. Ponchos were sometimes carried in the monsoon season, and in 1967 the lightweight poncho was issued, being less bulky and quieter but also less waterproof. Most teams carried at least one poncho to make a hasty litter. In some areas of Vietnam and during some seasons, comparatively cool nights were experienced. Poncho liners proved invaluable. Though a bit bulky, they were very light and comfortable. They consisted of a thin layer of polyester batting sewn between outer camouflage nylon and parachute cloth. They readily absorbed water but were much lighter than a wet wool blanket, and they dried more quickly.

Most men carried a knife, not so much as a weapon as a tool. One of the most common was the Air Force survival knife with a sharpening stone provided in a pocket on its leather sheath. Privately purchased fighting knifes were also popular, as were pocket knives.

Numerous items of air-ground marking gear were carried. From the air a small team was extremely difficult to locate when looking down on a vast, rugged jungle. The team had only a short range of vision and could identify few landmarks readily visible from the air. These aids included colored smoke grenades, signal mirrors, handheld signal panels, and at night, handheld colored "pop-up" flares, strobe lights, pen flares, and flashlights with colored lens. Marking one's position on the

LRPs often carried a sheath knife. Typical models were (left to right): Gerber Mk II fighting knife, Randall Model 16 fighting knife, and Air Force survival knife (with a 5-in. blade, for length comparison). All have sharpening stones in their sheath pockets. (Trey Moore collection)

LEFT
"Pop-ups" were used for signaling. Issued in a gray tube opened by a key and strip, the packing tube was discarded and the signal carried in the rucksack with the cap over the muzzle (left end). To fire it, the cap was slid onto the other end up to the red line, and then the cap slapped with the palm with the tube in a vertical position. A rocket propelled the signal to about 200m. The white star parachute provided good self-illumination. (Trey Moore collection)

BOTTOM LEFT
The larger type "pen flare gun," the A/P255-5A personal distress signal kit, could penetrate foliage better than the smaller M186 pen flare. This kit was provided with only red flares. (Trey Moore collection)

ground to friendly aircraft was essential, especially when attack helicopters and fighter-bombers were delivering ordnance at "danger close."[6] It was also necessary to mark helicopter pickup zones for extraction.

The actual gear carried by a LRP depended on his duties, team mission, terrain, weather, personal preferences, and unit SOP. How and where the gear was carried was sometimes specified by SOP, but more often according to individual preferences. Often, critical items to be carried were specified, so that

Individual gear

Weapons

5.56mm M16A1 rifle or XM177E2 submachine gun	1
Fragmentation grenades	4–6
M34 WP grenade and/or M7A2 CS grenade	1
M18A1 Claymore antipersonnel mine	1
Cleaning gear	1 set

Communications/air-ground signaling

M18 colored and/or minismoke grenades	1–4
"Pop-up" ground signal flares	1–2
Marker panel	1
Extra radio battery	1

Existence

LRP rations	2 per day of anticipated mission duration
1- and 2-qt water canteens	2–6
Canteen cup	1
Water purification tablets	1 bottle
Insect repellent	1 bottle
Foot powder	1 can
Poncho	1 or none
Poncho liner	1
Mosquito net (some areas/seasons)	1
Sleeping sweater (some areas/seasons)	1
Spare socks	1–2 pairs

Mission

Acetate-covered map of area of operation (AO)	1
Notepad and pencil	1
Lensatic compass (sometimes a spare button compass)	1
M49A1 trip flares	1–2
Camouflage stick	1
Rappelling seat rope (12–14ft)	1
Snap links	1–2
M1950 leather gloves	1 pair
Flotation vest (only in the Mekong Delta)	1
Medical items (varied greatly)	

The rigging arrangement for rappelling ropes, secured to floor cargo rings aboard a Huey, two per side. The log reduces rope chaffing. (US Army)

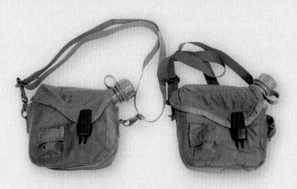

Typical items carried by a LRP, (left to right): Lensatic compass attached to the person by a dummy cord; wrist compass on an olive drab web band carried as a backup; SDU-5E strobe light; Mk 3 signal mirror (backside). (Trey Moore collection)

The flexible plastic 2-qt canteen proved to be more practical than the bladder type. The one to the left has a waterproofed case, and the one on the right has a nylon case. The carrying strap was usually removed, and it secured to the rucksack by slide hooks on the carrier's back. (Trey Moore collection)

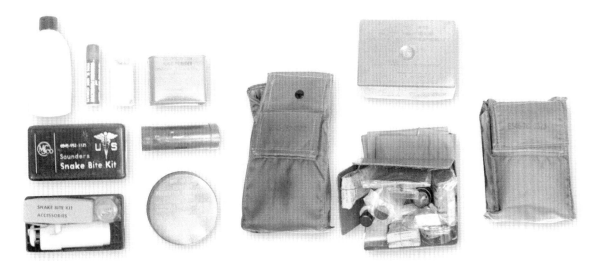

if the man became a casualty the equipment could be recovered quickly. While details varied, a LRP would typically carry the items listed in the box below.

Team equipment included radios, surveillance gear, air-ground signaling items, and special items needed to accomplish specific missions. These items were distributed as equally as possible among team members. Loads were invariably unequal with the radio operators especially burdened. In some teams each man carried one of the air-ground signaling items, but more often too few men were available. Two radios were carried as this was the LRPs' means of reporting timely information and was their lifeline for fire support and extraction. A backup was essential. Often one man was designated the team medic, although he had received only cursory training from company medics. He carried a medical kit with dressings, bandages, medications, and drugs. Other team members would carry additional dressings, morphine syrettes, and serum albumin cans.

Radios

The radio was the team's lifeline. The Korean War-era 26lb (11.8kg) AN/PRC-10, using vacuum tubes and having a three- to five-mile (5–8km) range, was

Team equipment

Team equipment was distributed between all members, and the number of items carried varied, depending on the mission. These are typical examples:

AN/PRC-25 or -77 radios	2
Survival radios	1–2
Olympus Pen EE 35mm camera	1
7x50 M17A1 binoculars	1–2
20x M49 observation telescope (occasionally)	1
AN/PVS-1 or -2 starlight scope (occasionally)	1
Mk III signal mirrors	2–4
SDU-5/E strobe lights	2–3
M186 pen flare projectors	2–3
MX-99/U or -991/U flashlights or penlights	2–3
Demolition materials (mission dependent)	
Extra ammunition for M79, M60, etc. for ambush missions	

An AN/PVS-1 "starlight scope" that could be mounted on an M14 or M16A1 rifle. These first-generation night vision weapons sights were heavy and of marginal effectiveness. (US Army)

used until 1967/68 when it was replaced by the solid-state AN/PRC-25. These 24.7lb (11.2kg) transistorized FM radios had only a five-mile range with the 3ft antenna. Using 10ft (3m) long whip antennas or jury-rigged "jungle antennas" and transmitting from high ground, they might reach 15 miles (24km). The similar AN/PRC-77 allowed the attachment of an AN/KY-57 secure voice device (cryptographic scrambler), but these were not used in the field to prevent their capture.

LRP base stations usually used AN/VRC-46, -47, and -48 radios, able to transmit on one frequency and receive on one, two, and three respectively. The RC-292 antenna ("Two-niner-two") was used by base stations. This was a sectionalized, up to 30ft (9m) tall, mast antenna supported by guy wires, and taller antenna towers were often erected.

LRPs used pocket-sized, handheld survival radios normally carried in aviators' survival vests. These served for short-range emergency contact with extraction helicopters and were especially valuable as they could be retained even if backpack radios were discarded or inoperational. These included the ACR/RT-10, AN/URC-64, and AN/PRC-90.

Weapons

LRPs required light, reliable weapons capable of laying down a good deal of firepower. Even on passive reconnaissance missions a team had to possess enough firepower to fight its

6 "Danger close;" the safe distance from friendly forces depends on the type of ordnance: helicopter machine guns – 100m; helicopter rockets – 200m, aerial bombs – 300m, mortars and artillery – 600m, naval guns 5in. and smaller – 750m, naval guns larger than 5in. – 1,000m. The ordnance may be adjusted in closer after the initial delivery.

The 5.56mm XM177E2 submachine gun was issued to many recon teams. Its compact design was ideal for use by LRPs. This is a 20-round magazine. Curved 30-round magazines were extremely rare. (US Army)

way out of a tight spot. Combat missions of course required more firepower, especially for a small team, but weaponry still had to be light. This was usually compensated for by increasing the size of teams. One school of thought held that teams should be armed with only personal defense weapons. Providing them with more firepower, such as M79 grenade launchers, would only lead teams to take aggressive action and compromise their mission. However, six men in enemy-controlled territory relying on slow-to-arrive helicopter extraction tend not to look for trouble regardless of how well they are armed.

The original TO&E called for 7.62mm M14 rifles, but they were heavy and only a limited amount of ammunition could be carried in their bulky 20-round magazines. Airborne and airmobile units arrived in Vietnam with the 5.56mm XM16E1 or M16A1 rifle and this became the standard rifle of LRP units. The selective-fire (650–750rpm) M16A1 weighed 6.3lb (2.8kg). From about 1968 some units obtained 5.56mm XM177E1 or XM177E2 submachine guns, short-barreled versions of the M16A1 with telescoping stocks and weighing 5.38lb (2.4kg).

The 40mm M79 shoulder-fired, single-shot grenade launcher weighed only 5.95lb (2.7kg) and allowed high-explosive rounds to be fired 493ft (150m) at point targets and 1,230ft (375m) for area fire. There was also a canister (buckshot) round with a 115ft (35m) range. Various pyrotechnic rounds (colored smoke and flares) were also available. LRP patrols were originally not authorized a so-called "thumper," although by 1969 it was standard issue. Some teams modified the M79, cutting down the barrel by 3in. (7.6cm), removing the rear sight, and sawing the butt stock off, leaving a pistol grip. It was carried on a cord or in a canvas holster. This provided a short-range emergency weapon for breaking contact. A man armed with a "blooper" would also carry a rifle. In 1967 a few units obtained XM148 grenade launchers and in 1968 they received the XM203 mounted under the M16A1 barrel. A 40mm grenade launcher gave a team an edge as they were effective at keeping the enemy down and disorganizing him. A rapid rate of high-explosive (HE) rounds confused the enemy and made him believe he had engaged a larger force, which was extremely valuable for ambushes.

Nonstandard weapons

A wide range of special purpose, nonstandard "exotic" weapons were used, but these generally saw only limited use. Units had their own rationale for using these weapons. They were acquired through trading with other US, Allied, and ARVN units, and some were requested under special allocations.

.30cal M2 selective-fire carbine
.45cal M3A1 submachine gun ("grease gun")
.45cal M1A1 submachine gun (Thompson)
7.62mm M14 rifle
7.62mm M21 sniper rifle
9mm Mk IIS silenced submachine gun (British Sten gun)
9mm m/45b submachine gun ("Swedish K") with or without silencer
.22cal HD pistol (Hi-Standard) with silencer
12-gauge pump shotguns*

*Typical models were the Remington Model 870, Ithaca Model 37, Savage Model 69E, and Stevens Model 77E with 20in. barrels.

Some teams carried one or two 5.2lb (2.4kg) single-shot M72 or M72A1 light antitank weapons (LAW): a 66mm HEAT rocket. These were used for ambushes and to break contact, especially against vehicles or sampans.

The M18A1 Claymore antipersonnel mine was a 3.5lb (1.6kg) directional mine in a rectangular, slightly curved fiberglass box with 1.5lb (0.7kg) of C4 backing 704 $^7/_{32}$in. (6mm) ball bearings, making them devastating to assaulting troops and those caught in ambush kill zones. It was electrically detonated by command, or it could be rigged with a tripwire to be activated by an intruder. When detonated the ball bearings were blasted out in a 60-degree fan with an optimum range of 164ft (50m), but dangerous out to 820ft (250m). Blast and secondary fragmentation were dangerous within 328ft (100m).

Hand grenades were important tools for self-defense and for breaking contact. The earlier "lemon grenades" included the M26, M26A1, M26A2,[7] M57, and M61, and they remained in use throughout the war. In 1967 the "baseball grenades" made their appearance; the M33, M59, M67, and M68. The M57, M61, M67, and M68 were identical to the M26A2, M26A1, M33, and M59, respectively, with the addition of safety clips. The wire clip was rotated to allow the arming lever to fly off once the arming pin was pulled and the grenade thrown. It helped prevent accidents if the grenade was inadvertently dropped.

M34 white phosphorous (WP) grenades were excellent break-contact weapons if they could be thrown far enough in vegetation. Besides creating an

 Sometimes .30cal M2 selective-fire carbines with 30-round magazines had the barrel cut down and the butt stock sawed off leaving a pistol grip, to use as a "spray and pray" break-contact weapon. (Author's collection)

---

7 The M26A2, M57, M59, and M68 were impact-fuzed grenades, which had the standard four-to five-second delay but would detonate before upon impact with the ground. Most troops refused to use them because they detonated if dropped or struck vegetation when thrown.

C **PATROL EQUIPMENT**

In 1968 the woodlands pattern camouflage jungle uniform began replacing tiger-stripes to provide a more functional, better-fitting uniform (1). Modernized nylon web gear also began to be issued. The nylon tropical rucksack, while an improvement over earlier options, was not large enough for the necessary amount of rations and gear. Every team member had to carry his share of team equipment, which was tailored to the mission and terrain. (2) Olympus Pen EE 35mm half-frame fixed focus camera. (3) 7x50 M17A1 binoculars with M44 leather case. "Binos" were often wrapped in cloth to prevent reflections. (4) 20x M49 observation telescope; seldom used as there were few opportunities for long-range observation. (5) AN/PVS-1 night vision sight introduced 1965. (6) AN/PVS-2 night vision sight, introduced 1967. "Starlight scopes" were in wider use by 1969. These were passive sights, which intensified moon and starlight rather than using infrared. Heavy and bulky (8lb and 6lb respectively), they saw limited use mounted on M14 or M16A1 rifles. (7) Mk III signal mirror for ground-air signaling. (8) SDU-5/E strobe light with a FG1C plastic flash guard to prevent it from being seen from the ground. The strobe could also flashed up an M79 grenade launcher barrel to shield it. (9) M186 pen flare projector with red, green, and white flares. They were not launched toward helicopters to prevent their being mistaken for tracers. (10) MX-991/U flashlight; the MX-99/U lacked the protective ears at the switch. Lens filters, stowed in an end cap, were available in green, amber, red, blackout, and diffusion. (11) XM28 lightweight protective mask was used in areas where tear gas had been spread. It was only effective for CS and not casualty-producing chemical agents. (12) BA-4386 battery for AN/PRC-25 and -77 radios. A spare was carried by each man. (13) ACR/RT-10 radio. (14) AN/URC-64 radio. (15) AN/PRC-90 radio; with flexible antenna folded and earphone case attached. One or two "survival radios" were carried by a team for emergency contact with extraction helicopters.

2

4

5

6

11

3

13

12

9

14

10

8

7

1

15

Two LRPs wearing XM29 tear gas protection masks. They have sewn skirt pockets from their woodlands pattern jungle fatigues on the shoulders. They use 1qt canteen carriers for their XM177E2 submachine gun magazines, which could hold five magazines. (US Army)

instantaneous smoke cloud they showered gobs and particles of burning WP up to 35m (115ft), making them dangerous to incautious throwers.

M7A2 and M7A3 riot control grenades were burning-type tear gas (CS) grenades, producing a cloud in 15–35 seconds. The AN-M8 white smoke grenade was also a burning type, creating a dense grayish-white cloud to screen movements and mark targets.

There were occasional attempts to shorten M14 rifles, M60 machine guns, and M2 carbines to reduce their weight and bulk, making them handier in close terrain. These shortened weapons were notoriously inaccurate and created a great deal of muzzle blast, noise, and recoil. They were strictly "spray and pray" weapons of marginal effectiveness.

Occasionally some teams were fully armed, or at least the pointman was armed with weapons employed by the VC/NVA. This was so that the firing signature would not alert the enemy to the team's presence, and it allowed captured ammunition to be used. These weapons included the 7.62mm AK-47, AKM and AKMS assault rifles; SKS carbine; and Czechoslovak vz.58 assault rifle. Use of such weapons was hampered by the lack of repair parts, insufficient magazines, and reliable ammunition.[8]

Some LRPs obtained .45cal M1911A1 Colt pistols and .38 Special Smith & Wesson Model 10 revolvers (issued to aviators). Privately owned 9mm and .45cal pistols, and .38 Special and .357 Magnum revolvers were popular. These unauthorized handguns were passed on or sold to buddies when the owners returned home.

8 Unknown to LRPs and their higher headquarters, MACV-SOG teams were "salting" VC/NVA ammunition dumps with exploding cartridges, which could make their way into Allied hands if captured. MACV directives discouraged the use of captured weapons for this reason.

9 The designations and assignments of LRP/Ranger units are discussed in Osprey Elite 13, *US Army Rangers and LRRP Units 1942–87.*

10 The two field force LRP companies were commanded by majors; not because they were a little larger than others but to allow the CO to more effectively work with senior staff officers.

CONDITIONS OF SERVICE

Volunteers assigned to a LRP company or detachment found a unit very different from the infantry rifle company, known colloquially as a "line company." A line company possessed a ten-man headquarters, three 41-man rifle platoons with three rifle squads and a weapons squad, and a weapons platoon (the latter usually deleted in Vietnam).

A LRP company was organized along very different lines.[9] They were more self-contained, although they were normally attached to another unit for administrative, mess, and military justice support. They were often attached to the divisional armored or air cavalry squadron or a brigade armored cavalry troop. The division/brigade retained operational control. An advantage of attaching LRPs to cavalry squadrons was that they had organic helicopter support for insertion and extraction, easing coordination. Additionally, the squadron's aero rifle platoon could be used as a reaction force.

The company HQ varied in size. The HQ section contained a captain company CO,[10] a first lieutenant executive officer (XO), a first sergeant, a supply sergeant, an armorer, a clerk or two, a couple of drivers, and perhaps a medic or two. A mess team with a mess sergeant and two to four cooks may or may not have been assigned, depending on the messing arrangements of the unit they were attached to. The operations and intelligence (O&I) section was assigned a captain or lieutenant operations officer, a lieutenant intelligence officer, operations and intelligence sergeants, an assistant operations sergeant, and a few enlisted operations assistants, intelligence analysts, and order of battle specialists. The transportation and maintenance section provided drivers and mechanics. Most units lacked this element, relying on their parent unit for their minimal transportation needs. Most companies possessed two to four ¼-ton M151A1 utility trucks ("jeeps"), perhaps a ¾-ton M37B1 cargo truck and one or two 2½-ton M35A1 cargo trucks. Brigade detachments/companies likely had only one to three vehicles.

Ideally a LRP company had a communications platoon with a large HQ manning the message center and containing radio repairmen, plus three base radio stations. These were intended to operate widely scattered stations, with all three monitoring all teams' frequencies. Very high frequency (VHF) amplitude-modulated (AM) radios were used that transmitted by skipping radio waves off the ionosphere. One or all stations might receive team messages depending on atmospheric conditions. The messages were transmitted by high-speed data burst and recorded by the base stations, which slowed down the recordings, transcribed them, and transmitted them to the company message center by radio teletype. The message center decrypted the messages and passed them to the O&I section. Intelligence information was then passed to the LRP company's division/brigade G2/S2 section where the information was analyzed, processed, and disseminated.

However, in Vietnam this advanced communications system was not used. The equipment was not available, and there was no time for the lengthy training of Morse code radio operators. For the most part, only line-of-sight frequency-modulated (FM) voice radios were used, although their range was greatly limited. This resulted in companies having only an eight- to twelve-man communications section to transmit and receive voice traffic to and from teams and to operate the message center.

The number of patrol platoons varied. The 61-man brigade LRP detachments (called companies from 1969) had one platoon. The 118-man divisional companies had two platoons while the 1st Cavalry Division's 198-man company had three. The two corps-level 230-man field force companies had four platoons.

The platoon HQ typically possessed only a lieutenant, a platoon sergeant, and an enlisted man described as a radio-telephone operator/driver, although he usually did neither; he was simply an assistant. The standard called for eight five-man patrols or teams per platoon. In reality there could be five to nine patrols/teams, with six to eight being common. The number of teams varied over time in any given unit owing to available personnel and reductions forced by casualties, illness, rotations, and personnel attending training or on leave.

A team, sometimes called a "recon team" (RT), was officially a "patrol." It was actually a squad echelon unit, but it would have been misleading to call it such because of its small size. "Squad" denoted an offensive maneuver unit. The term "patrol" had its origins with the British Special Air Service and was adopted by NATO LRPs including those of the United States. "Team" was a more familiar term to Americans, implying a small, close-knit group cooperating with one another. Officially a patrol was comprised of five men: patrol leader (staff

D THE RECON TEAM

The final inspection was conducted just prior to boarding the helicopter to ensure all weapons and equipment were ready and present, that gear was properly secured and silenced, and that camouflage was applied. The TL (2) will also ask questions of his men to assess their state of readiness. The pointman (1), here with a Winchester Model 1200 trench gun along with his slung M16A1, is the most experienced man, but the assistant TL might serve as a pointman, with a scout as the "tail gunner." The radio operator (3) carries an AN/PRC-10 in his rucksack, as does the TL. It was common for the TL or the assistant to carry a radio in teams of five men and smaller. The second scout (4) doubles as the team medic, carrying additional medical gear in his ruck. He is also armed with a cut-down M79 grenade launcher. The assistant TL (5) here serves as the "tail gunner" bringing up the team's rear. Part of mission preparation was to learn who carried what team equipment and where it was carried, so that it could be recovered if necessary.

sergeant), assistant patrol leader (sergeant), senior scout/observer (specialist 4), senior radio operator (specialist 4), and scout/observer (private first class). More commonly in Vietnam a sixth man was added, either another radio operator or a scout/observer (private first class). Patrol leaders were commonly called team leaders (TL). Six men gave the team another weapon, another pair of eyes, and a body to share watch. The Ranger Course concept of always having two men work as "Ranger buddies" was a strong inducement for even-number-strength teams. They were to watch out for one another and share the burdens. While five- or six-man teams were common, three- and four-man teams were sometimes employed. For ambushes, prisoner snatches, recovery, and other offensive operations, teams as large as 12 men might be employed as a "heavy team." This might be achieved by combining two "light teams" under the senior or most capable leader, or pulling selected individuals with specific expertise from other teams. On occasion a platoon leader or sergeant might lead a heavy team. The 9th Infantry Division's LRP company, operating in the canal-crisscrossed Mekong Delta, used eight-man teams with four going into each of its two 16ft (4.9m) plastic assault boats. Teams were usually designated by two-digit numbers, the first identifying the platoon and the second identifying the team within the platoon (11 = 1st Platoon, Patrol 1; 36 = 3rd Platoon, Patrol 6). Other numbering systems were used, and some were designated by state or other names.

In 1966–67 the 4th Infantry Division employed three brigade LRRP detachments of eight five-man Recondo teams and three Hawkeye teams.[11] The latter were composed of two Americans and two Montagnards who had undergone a ten-day training program. Recondo teams performed as normal LRPs while the Hawkeyes intercepted enemy couriers and hampered enemy scouting and surveillance efforts. A division Recondo Detachment of the same organization was assigned to the cavalry squadron. Other divisions sometimes attached their company's platoons directly to brigades.

Ideally, patrols developed into tight-knit teams that developed a deep trust in one another, anticipated their teammates' actions, knew their capabilities and limitations, and shared a hooch and off-duty hours. They could recognize one another's silhouettes in the dim jungle and even the gait of their walk from a distance. Assembling new teams after suffering casualties or the turnover of personnel was a slow process. New members had to be trained and accepted. Sometimes a man did not fit into a team; each team had its own personality, and was tried out by others.

It is worth noting that the early provisional LRP units were much smaller and possessed the bare minimum of support personnel. Often they were of platoon size with three to nine patrols. Provisional units were formed from assets drawn from other units of the parent command. That means every man, weapon, vehicle, radio, typewriter, and rucksack was given up by

11 "Recondo" was coined by General Westmoreland when commanding the 101st Airborne Division in 1959 and is a contraction of "Reconnaissance" and "commando." Two- to three-week Recondo courses were conducted by some divisions as "mini-Ranger" courses. "Hawkeye" is an old frontier scout and hunting term for a sharp-eyed person.

12 The 75th Infantry carried the consolidated lineages of the 5307th Composite Unit (Provisional) – Merrill's Marauders – and the 475th Infantry Regiment (Special), which had continued the Marauders' long-range penetration mission in Burma. In 1974 the new Ranger battalions were assigned the 75th Infantry lineage and those of Vietnam Ranger companies. The 75th did not then carry the lineages of the World War II Ranger battalions and Korean War Ranger companies, which had been assigned to Special Forces in 1960. In 1986 those unit's lineages were withdrawn from the 1st Special Forces lineage and consolidated with the 75th Infantry.

another unit. The provisional unit commander may have had command authority, but the troops' accountability, ration allocation, military justice, and pay were the responsibility of the individual's original assigned unit.

The first small provisional LRP units bore names such as 173nd Airborne Brigade LRRP Platoon and Detachment A (LRP) (Provisional), 196th Infantry Brigade. MACV authorized the formation of such units on July 8, 1966. On December 20, 1967, the Army authorized the establishment of permanent LRP field force and divisional companies and brigade detachments with assigned lineages. This is when the units were provided formal TO&Es and given the lineages of infantry units. On February 1, 1969, these companies and detachments were redesignated as Ranger companies and assigned the lineage of the 75th Infantry.[12]

BELIEF AND BELONGING

"Highly motivated" are the words that best sum up the most desirable trait of a LRP. But no one trait can truly describe a LRP. Militarily proficient, technically competent, dependable, patient, courageous, physically fit, self-starter, and other terms can describe the necessary qualities of a LRP. But to achieve any of these and prevail under demanding circumstances required a highly motivated individual.

No aptitude tests, interviews, or observation during training effectively assessed how a man would actually perform in combat, although airborne training was a good indication of a soldier's ability to deal with stress as well as acquiring new skills. The demands made on individuals to pull their weight and perform effectively and reliably as part of the team were just as critical to a mission's success, even if no contact with the enemy was made, as how they performed under the stress of combat.

There are many intangibles that affect and strengthen a soldier's qualities. Such qualities may be found in the "ideal" soldier, if there is any such thing, but they are also found in the less-than-ideal soldier. There have always been soldiers who rebel against authority, show disrespect or at least disregard for some superiors, possess a "rebel" streak, and display a degree of wildness or at least less-than-model behavior. With the right leadership, both by example and direction, such individuals performed effectively. The downside was that the image they created led outsiders to assume them to be typical of LRPs. The units sometimes gained an undeserved reputation owing to the actions of a few individuals coming across as overly cocky, arrogant, or just plain crazy.

An intangible enhancing of a soldier's qualities is the benefit of a good esprit de corps. Simply *belonging* to a LRP or other special unit is not enough; a unit is not "elite" simply because someone says it is. That distinction had to be earned, not only by its present actions or reputation, but reinforced by its ties to the past. While most LRPs were not parachute-qualified, the airborne mystique contributed a great deal to unit spirit. Airborne training was the only course in the Army in which enlisted men and officers went through exactly the same training together. (The same can be said of Ranger training, but it was rare for enlisted men at the time to attend.) Airborne units effectively used their history, traditions, and image to enhance their esprit de corps. They bore a proud record from World War II and were considered elite in their own right, although the view was held begrudgingly by "legs." Airborne units in Vietnam boasted a none-too-shabby reputation themselves. Their jump wings,

jump boots, and other trappings were jealously protected and flaunted, and they were enthusiastically vocal in letting others know who they were. Raucous airborne songs, Jody chants, and even their greetings constantly reminded everyone within earshot they were paratroopers. When an airborne soldier greeted and saluted an officer, airborne or otherwise, he would shout, "Airborne, Sir!" An airborne officer would reply, "All the way!" while a leg officer might simply mutter, "Good morning, soldier" or "As you were."

When the companies were redesignated Ranger in 1969, whether airborne-qualified or not, the units now could claim a common Ranger linkage that dated back to colonial America. Their greeting now was "Rangers lead the way!" They had a common lineage through the 75th Infantry that included Merrill's Marauders and, even though they had no direct lineage with the World War II and Korean War Rangers, they shared their traditions. Few actually attended the Ranger Course, but they embraced the Rangers' image of excellence, the black beret, and other trappings.

And yet there was another factor in play for these men. They believed in the LRP concept and that their sacrifices were worth the effort to find the enemy. This belief did not always extend to other branches of the forces. Some questioned the value of LRP intelligence collection efforts (unless they were processing, analyzing, and receiving that intelligence), felt they siphoned off too many scarce manpower resources, and begrudged them their notoriety and apparent self-aggrandizing. LRPs were especially disliked by line company officers who thought they received too much credit when their own companies were risking life and limb daily. At times, these were the companies that had to break brush and disregard movement security when ordered to make all haste cross-country to rescue an engaged LRP team.

There is little doubt that LRPs were boastful, highly strung, and quickly rose to any challenge to their image in base clubs. But most of all, they can be characterized by their admirable loyalty to their team. These were the men that a LRP knew he could count on. LRPs put up with some commanders who disbelieved their intelligence reports (often owing to their own

LRP and Ranger units attracted a more independent and adventurous soldier, but he had to be a part of the small, close-knit team. (Trey Moore collection)

preferences or preconceived notions of the LRPs), "friendly" helicopters attacking them, inaccurate or late fire support, delayed extraction helicopters, and the "chickenshit" they had to deal with in base. Yet none of that really mattered so long as they could rely on their team.

ON CAMPAIGN

Deployment to LRP units

Future LRPs deployed to Vietnam in the same way as any other infantryman. They were processed at one of two replacement battalions, underwent the division's/brigade's orientation course to become acclimatized, and were assigned to an infantry battalion. Records were screened, and those with Ranger training or who had previous LRP or Special Forces experience were asked to volunteer for LRPs. At some point, infantrymen with the desire volunteered for the LRPs. Upon acceptance, they underwent the unit's training program regardless of previous experience. Every unit had its own techniques of operations, and the training program was an opportunity for unit leaders to assess the individual.

Some individuals were selected to attend the MACV Recondo School. This three-week course was conducted by Project Delta, a 5th Special Forces Group special reconnaissance project at Nha Trang. It was established in September 1966 to train its own personnel, but General Westmoreland directed the school to provide training for US and allied LRP units. The demanding course provided 288 hours of classroom and field instruction. On average about 20 members of a 60-student class washed out. LRP units might send individuals or a complete team for training to fill their quotas. However, units were fortunate if one out of five members was able to attend the course. Students reported with their weapon, web gear, and a basic load of ammunition and grenades. They were provided a 30lb (13.6kg) sandbag, which they carried in their rucksack at all times along with other gear and four full canteens. Morning calisthenics were conducted, along with marches starting at two miles (3.2km) and increasing to seven miles (11.3km) in 90 minutes. Five-man teams were formed, led by instructors. The first week was classroom instruction in the compound. The second week was mostly conducted in nearby training areas and ranges,

ABOVE LEFT
A MACV Recondo School instructor (the Recondo patch can be seen on his right breast pocket) explains to LRP students how to rig rappelling ropes in a helicopter. (John Burford collection)

ABOVE
A soldier practices rappelling from a 40ft tower prior to doing it from a hovering helicopter. Helmets were worn during training, but LRPs rappelled bareheaded during actual insertions. (US Army)

Two Special Forces instructors at the MACV Recondo School display the STABO harness. The man to the left has the leg straps fastened while the man to the left has them secured by tape to the back straps, as would be worn when patrolling. (US Army)

where practical exercises and techniques were covered. The third week was an instructor-led patrol mission in a relatively secure area. Some 3,000 US personnel were trained by the MACV Recondo School. Its impact was broad, in that graduates passed on their skills to their own units and based their own training on the Recondo's.

Living conditions on base

LRP units were located at division or brigade base camps, which were comparatively secure, enduring only an occasional rocket or mortar attack. Units usually lived in one- or two-story temporary wooden barracks with bunks and mattresses, or at least folding cots with a nylon bed and an air mattress, and a mosquito net. A camouflaged poncho liner served as bed linen and blanket. Division/brigade bases sometimes relocated, and the troops would live under canvas. The bases were notoriously dusty in the dry season, and the dust

Recondo School program of instruction

Subject	Time (hours:minutes)
Administration	15:00
Physical fitness	14:20
Medical	3:30
Communications	8:30
Intelligence	4:40
Patrol exercises	62:40
Weapons instruction	15:10
Air operations	18:30
Land navigation	15:30
Examinations, critiques	6:30
Commander's time	13:00
Practical patrol mission	112:40

At the MACV Recondo School, two students demonstrate lifting off in McGuire rigs by a helicopter. It was a less-than-comfortable ride. All have removed their headgear to avoid it being blown off by the hovering helicopter. (US Army)

Three LRPs are lifted out during training in McGuire rigs. Normally their rucksacks would be snap-linked to D-rings on the straps.

Base camp living conditions were often Spartan, as seen here at the H/75th Infantry with sandbag-protected tents and bunkers in which shelter was taken during rocket and mortar attacks. (John Burford collection)

permeated everything. During the monsoon season the dust was replaced by glutinous mud. Local "hooch maids" performed menial duties such as cleaning the quarters and laundering uniforms. Officially they were hands-off sexually, but this did not keep some girls from freelancing. Latrines, showers, and washrooms were separate buildings. The mess halls served rations little different from those served in Stateside messes. The bases boasted clubs, outdoor movie theaters, Armed Forces Television Network showing old TV shows, United States Organization (USO) shows, recreational activities, and medical and dental clinics. LRPs typically kept to themselves and did not socialize with the the support personnel – so-called rear echelon mother***kers (REMFs) – or even other infantry units.

A crude field shower facility. The 3-gallon canvas shower bag was tuned on and off by turning the large shower head, which surprisingly built up more than adequate water pressure. A good shower could be had with just 4-5 gallons. (John Burford collection)

Divisional brigade bases were sometimes more temporary, and patrol platoons or recon teams might operate from these and battalion firebases as forward operating bases (FOB), placing them closer to their AO. Teams would be rotated to these Spartan FOBs.

Meals consisted of B-rations: canned, dehydrated, and preserved foods, mostly in #10 (1-gallon) cans. Some A-rations – fresh and frozen foods (mostly steaks, pork chops, chicken, and fish) were served, and bread was baked in base bakeries. Iced tea, fruit juice, reconstituted milk, "bug juice" (questionable fruit punch), and coffee were also served. Eggs were mostly powdered. Some fresh vegetables and canned fruits were available.

Planning and types of missions

The company headquarters consisted of an orderly room, operations and communication bunkers, and a supply room. The ops bunker, or TOC, was where missions were planned and monitored, and where committed teams were briefed and debriefed upon

The base camp of Company F (LRP), 58th Infantry of the 101st Airborne Division, 1968. This unit was redesignated Company L (Ranger), 75th Infantry at the beginning of 1969. (John Burford collection)

their return. The comms center held banks of radios that monitored each team's frequency, recorded every message and passed the information to the TOC, and forwarded intelligence to the division/brigade G2/S2.

The patrol platoons were responsible for the training, readiness, and administration of recon teams. They did not operate as platoons; rather the teams were committed on independent missions under company control. Platoon commanders and sergeants assisted teams in planning missions, developed preplotted artillery and mission overlays, participated in premission briefings, undertook reconnaissance overflights with team leaders, and flew

RECONDO SCHOOL, NHA TRANG, RVN

There were three systems available to extract recon teams when helicopters were unable to land on the PZ. The McGuire rig was developed by SF Sergeant Major Charles T. McGuire of Project Delta. This was a system of three 120ft 5/8in nylon ropes suspended from one side of a Huey. The ropes were stowed in a paratrooper's weapons container with the harness and a sandbag. They were dropped out of the chopper and three LRPs attached their rucksacks, stepped into the loop (8ft A7A nylon strap), adjusted it, slipped their left hand into a wrist loop, and the chopper lifted off. They could not be hoisted into the chopper, but were flown back to base dangling below the bird, unless a secure clearing was found to land and take them aboard. The harness was extremely uncomfortable on a long flight and there was danger of a wounded man falling. The STABO harness was developed by SF Major Robert L. Stevens, Captain John. D.H. Knabb, and Sgt 1st Class Clifford L. Roberts, all of Project Delta. The harness was designed to be worn with web gear. Its leg straps were rolled up and secured by tape or rubber bands until needed. Ropes were dropped in the same manner as the McGuire, but had two snap-hooks on the ends that clipped into D-rings on the harness shoulders. The STABO was available to LRPs in late 1970. Another system was an 80ft ladder with tubular aluminum rungs on thin steel cables. Soldiers could climb into a hovering helicopter and be lifted out clinging to it. Here a MACV Recondo School instructor describes the STABO harness and McGuire rig to LRP students. The MACV Recondo School insignia was awarded to graduates for wear as a pocket patch.

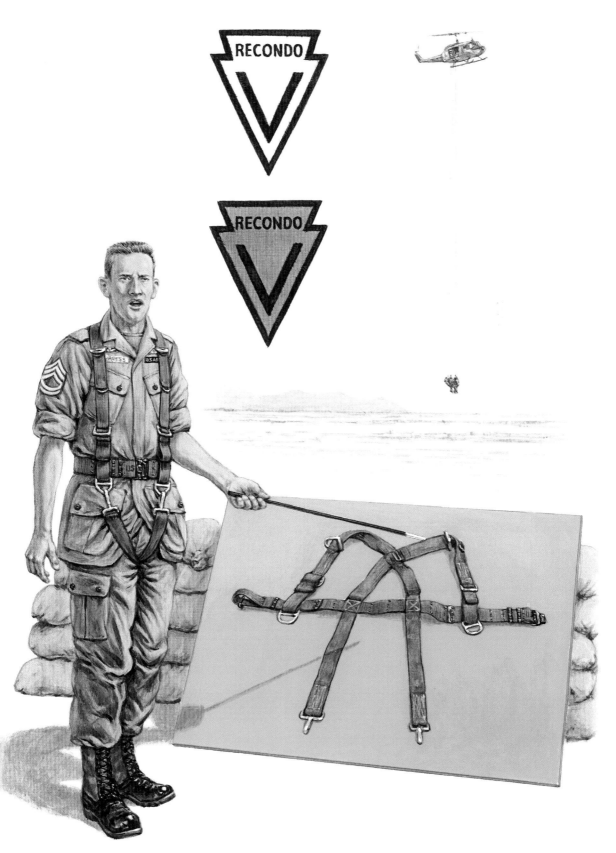

A main mission of LRPs was to locate and explore VC trails, which as can be seen, were virtually undetectable from the air and only found on the ground by running across one underfoot. (US Army)

aboard insertion and extraction helicopters or in C&C (command and control) birds aiding the location of the LZ/PZ (pickup zone). They seldom if ever accompanied patrols. When they did it was as a sixth member rather than leading it. They might do so to access terrain and operating conditions in a new AO, assess the team, or simply to earn a CIB.

The company commander and operations officer oversaw mission planning, maintained liaison with controlling headquarters, issued orders for team insertion and extraction, and flew in the C&C bird during insertions and extractions, as well as responding to team contacts arriving on-station with gunships, closely monitoring missions, and approving/rejecting changes to missions, requests for extraction, and coordinating fire support.

While it can be said that the primary mission of LRPs was intelligence collection, with combat patrols being a secondary mission, a great variety of missions were conducted. The various kinds of missions are detailed below.

Reconnaissance missions
Covert reconnaissance of specified points, areas, and routes
Surveillance of enemy infiltration routes and base areas
Terrain analysis and map corrections
Canal and river reconnaissance
Locating and plotting trail systems
Confirming sightings of enemy forces reported by aerial reconnaissance
Reconnaissance of potential LZs for larger forces
Prolonged surveillance of planned LZ for larger forces
Luring enemy forces to a particular point followed by extraction and replacement by larger forces
Conducting bomb damage assessment of areas struck by B-52s
Searching for enemy rocket-launching sites outside bases
Recovering dead, weapons, radios, etc. from downed aircraft
Emplacing unattended ground movement sensors
Operating radio relay sites for other teams

Combat missions
Reaction teams for downed helicopters
Rapid reinforcement of outposts
Local ambush patrols for base security
Countering enemy patrols near US bases
Conducting prisoner snatches
Executing small-scale raids on enemy sites
Screening the flanks and rear of larger moving units to counter enemy patrols
Direct air and artillery strikes on discovered enemy forces/facilities
Security for sniper teams
Security for underwater demolition and explosive ordnance disposal teams
Emplacing antipersonnel or antivehicle mines on roads and trails

Often LRP teams were delivered to a remote temporary firebase and then would depart on foot at dusk or before dawn. To the left a LRP can be seen with a serum albumin can taped to the back shoulder yoke of his suspenders. This was a blood volume expander that saved many lives. (US Army)

A LRP team loads into a Huey for mission insertion. A helicopter crew chief (wearing a baseball cap) assists with the on-load. (John Burford collection)

It must be emphasized that specific LRP units conducted different types of missions at different times. This was affected by the nature of the enemy, the civilian population, terrain, and the preferences of commanders. Some commanders used their LRPs solely for covert reconnaissance while others focused on small-scale combat and reaction force missions. This focus changed as commanders changed. However, it was realized that to ensure success a team was assigned either a reconnaissance or a combat mission, not both.

If at all possible teams were allowed at least a 36-hour standdown between missions. Continuous back-to-back missions with inadequate rest wore down a team and led to mistakes and inefficiency. Occasionally, operational tempo did not allow this luxury, but during lulls in missions, teams undertook individual and team training, reinforcing or learning new skills.

LRP rats

The "food packet, long range patrol" – "LRP rations" – were introduced in 1965 for small teams. They were designed to be light, compact, nourishing, and filling. These were the first freeze-dried rations issued by the Army and the predecessor of the modern army-issue meal, ready-to-eat (MRE). Early-issue packets were packaged in olive drab foil-lined waterproofed cotton. Later issues were in heavy, olive drab plastic bags. Freeze-drying removed 100 percent of the moisture (a meal contained 70–90 percent water) resulting in about an 11-ounce (4,812 gram) packet averaging 1,100 calories. Troops could subsist on them for up to ten days. The main course was a precooked, freeze-dried block of food contained in a clear plastic bag with a white square cardboard stiffener on the bottom. This packet was sealed in a dark brown foil bag. A few ounces of cold or hot water were added, the bag folded shut, and the food kneaded to completely mix the water. It could be eaten dry on the move, precluding cooking odors. A chocolate, coconut, or vanilla wafer ("John Wayne bar");

orange-flavored cereal; or fruitcake bar was included along with two packets of bitter instant coffee, clumpy powdered nondairy creamer, and sugar. Also provided were a white plastic spoon, a small roll of toilet paper, matchbook, and a soft wooden toothpick for cleaning teeth, all held in a dark brown foil accessory packet. No cigarettes were provided as they were in C-rations – smoking was not permitted on patrol for obvious reasons. Forty meals were packed in a case. Opinions differed, but menus Nos. 3, 5, and 8 were generally popular with Nos. 1 and 6 being the least popular. No. 2 was good, but one had to be cautious of the stray bean failing to absorb water that could break a tooth. The packets included:

No. 1 Beef hash
No. 2 Chili con carne
No. 3 Spaghetti with
    meat sauce
No. 4 Beef with rice

No. 5 Chicken stew
No. 6 Escalloped potatoes
    with ham
No. 7 Beef stew
No. 8 Chicken with rice

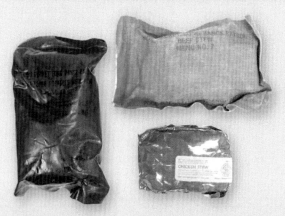

A "food packet, long range patrol," or "LRP ration." To the left is the later brown plastic bag and to the upper right is the earlier foil-backed cloth bag. The smaller brown bag to the lower right is the main course meal. (Trey Moore collection)

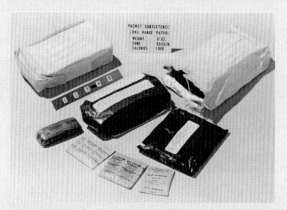

An early-issue LRP ration (left to right): sealed ration, main course packet, cocoa powder packet, coconut bar, instant coffee, dry cream product, and sugar packets. (US Army)

EXPERIENCE IN BATTLE

No two missions were the same: units operated differently, and the terrain, weather, and enemy and civilian situations caused even more variation. The preinfiltration phase was extremely important. Effective planning and preparation went a long way to achieving mission success. LRPs' primary mission was to collect and report battlefield intelligence information. The most successful LRP missions were those on which not a single shot was fired. They searched for, located, and reported the enemy. They might direct artillery or air strikes on him, move into the target area, conduct a battle damage assessment, and report the results. Thus, a six-man patrol had the potential to kill more of the enemy than a rifle company could.

Missions were assigned by the division/brigade G2/S2 specifying the AO, purpose, and dates. Many other details were required, including insertion time, means of delivery, enemy and friendly forces in the area, fire support, weather forecast, exactly what information was to be collected, extraction date/time/means, and more. Many details had to be worked out during the planning process involving the O&I section, division/brigade G2/S2 and G2/S3, LRP communications element, supporting aviation[13] and artillery units, and the team itself. Missions were from one to six days and AOs might be 1.5 square miles (4 square kilometers) or smaller. AOs were designated "No fire, no fly zones" where no artillery could be fired and no helicopters allowed to overfly unless supporting the mission. Teams were not resupplied to extend missions as this would compromise their location. If it was necessary to keep a team in the AO, the current team was extracted and a fresh one inserted at the same time – "direct exchange" (DX) – either there or elsewhere in the AO.

Mission preparation

The LRP team received a warning order 24–48 hours prior to insertion. Teams had well-developed SOPs and preparations were fairly routine. When alerted the team would not bathe or use scented soap, shampoo, or aftershave lotion. Such alien scents were easily detected by the VC/NVA. The TL and sometimes his assistant or even the entire team were briefed either by representatives of the division/brigade G2/S2 and G2/S3 section or the LRP operations and intelligence officers. Weapons were cleaned and test-fired, then cleaned without disassembly. Ammunition, grenades, pyrotechnics, rations, radio batteries, expendable supplies (medical items, water purification tablets, insect repellent), and any special items of equipment were drawn. The radio operators did a commo check and received call signs and frequencies (primary, alternate, aviation, artillery). Everything was carefully checked and packed. Coordination was continuous as the plan developed and the inevitable changes were made.

Much attention was given to the insertion plan. LRPs did not conduct local patrols, as infantry units could handle that. LRPs operated in remote, denied areas. It was not a matter of merely walking out of a firebase, although that sometimes occurred if a remote base was situated in the right area. Stay-behind insertions were also conducted. The team might accompany a rifle company that was air-assaulted into an LZ. The team could break off and move in another direction or the company would be extracted from a PZ after just hours on the ground, to be reinserted elsewhere, and the team would remain. The same was done during airmobile artillery raids. A howitzer battery was inserted on a hilltop, fired on preplotted targets, and departed, leaving the team behind. A team might also ride into an area aboard a mechanized unit's armored personnel carriers or on riverine craft in the Delta, and be dropped off as the unit moved on.

Helicopter was by far the most common means of insertion. A primary LZ and one or two alternates were selected. This was difficult in some areas due to the scarcity of viable LZs. A danger in such areas was that the enemy could easily place surveillance, often just a village boy who would alert the local VC. When LZs were unavailable or could be under surveillance, a team might rappel in through sparse tree growth, using ropes from as high as 100ft (30m). More commonly the team would disembark from a landed or hovering helicopter a few feet off the ground, carefully avoiding flooding and rocks, stumps, and logs hidden in vegetation.

Once briefed, team preparations continued, which included practicing movement formations, immediate action drills, and disembarking the helicopter,

13 See Osprey Elite 154, *Vietnam Airmobile Warfare Tactics*.

Rather than large multiple helicopter landings zones, LRPs preferred small discreet LZs such as this bomb-blasted clearing. (US Army)

especially if rappelling. Even if they had just completed a mission, such rehearsals served to put LRPs in the necessary frame of mind. The team studied the AO map and aerial photographs, identified LZs and PZs, plotted artillery target reference points, and their route and objectives. If at all possible the TL and a unit officer conducted a reconnaissance overflight of the AO, identifying the LZs and route. Such flights did not orbit or hover over points of interest, but merely overflew the area. Their findings might result in further changes.

The team would then present a briefback of all aspects of their mission to the company commander and operations officer. Questions were asked to ensure the team was fully prepared to accomplish the mission and deal with unforeseen situations. The TL would conduct a final inspection ensuring all weapons and equipment were on hand and ready, that equipment was properly secured and silenced, and that all camouflage measures taken.

Noise discipline was critical, and all gear with the potential of making noise was taped or padded – "taping up" – especially buckles and snaps. Rifle sling swivels were removed along with the unnecessary sling. No metal-on-metal contact was permitted when packing equipment. Small items might be padded by placing them in a sock. Rations were "broken down:" the meal components were removed from the outer packaging and undesired items discarded to reduce weight and bulk. LRP rations were not always available, and C-rations were often substituted. These canned rations were heavier, made more noise when opening, and caused stronger food odors, plus the cans had to be disposed of. Usually only the meat and fruit cans were retained and packed in socks, while the B units (cookies, "John Wayne crackers," cocoa power) were discarded.

It was also essential to waterproof items from rain, sweat, and wading streams. Plastic sandwich bags had been introduced in 1957 but were scarce in Vietnam and the ziplock bag, introduced in 1968, was even rarer. Soldiers made do with the plastic, foil, or cellophane bags from rations and batteries. The only documentation they carried, if any, was their ID and Geneva Convention cards. A small notebook was carried for recording information

with a pencil, as pen ink became illegible if the paper got wet. A Signal Operating Instruction (SOI) extract was carried. This included radio call signs, frequencies, and encryption codes. Radio handsets were plastic-bagged to protect from water and dust; a spare handset was sometimes carried. Maps were covered with "combat acetate" or "sticky acetate" on both sides. This was a thinner, more flexible plastic than the heavier, nonsticking acetate used as map overlays in command posts. It had adhesive on one side, allowing it to be applied to a map sheet. This was more to protect the map from water than for grease pencil marking. No mission data was marked on maps, to deny the enemy information if captured. Yet maps might be annotated with updated information discovered by the team along with enemy information. Each man carried a map in the event he became separated from the rest of the team.

Each round of ammunition was cleaned and carefully loaded, with 18 per magazine to prevent straining the spring. The third round from the bottom might be tracer to alert the firer that he was almost empty. Some men carried a magazine or two of all tracers (this does not harm the weapon as some claim)

BELOW
Ammunition used in common LRP weapons (left to right): 7.62mm NATO (M14 rifle, M60 machine gun), 5.56mm (M16A1 rifle, XM177-series submachine guns), .30cal carbine (M2 carbine), .45cal Colt (M1911A1 pistol), 9mm Parabellum (various unofficial pistols and submachine guns), and 7.62mm Soviet short (AK assault rifles. No Soviet 7.62mm rounds were interchangeable with the 7.62mm NATO as was rumored). (Author's collection)

A LRP team rapidly off-loads from a UH-1H Huey without it fully touching down. The team could be out of the slick and it would be on its way in less than five seconds. Note the team members have removed their boonie hats to prevent them from being blown away. (John Burford collection)

or every other round a tracer. This was carried by the pointman and used to break contact, making it appear to the enemy they were under heavier fire. Magazines were inserted in pouches mouth down and bullets pointing away from the body, with a tape tab affixed to the magazines' bottoms to aid extraction from the pouch. A second magazine was often taped to the magazine in the weapon for quick change. Grenade levers were taped prior to the introduction of safety clips, or arming rings were taped to prevent them from snagging on vegetation. Trip flares and "pop-ups" were removed from packaging, and Claymores were rigged with short delay fuzes and packed in the tops of rucksacks for quick access to leave on the backtrail.

The team loaded aboard the Huey with the TL on the side they planned to disembark from. They would sit down on the LZ close to a wood line for them to rush into. Normal rules were for weapons to be empty, but a LRP team went in locked and loaded with weapons on "safe." With the seats removed they sat on the floor without seatbelts, with muzzles down and hats in pockets to prevent them from being blown away. Ideally the team riding in the insertion chopper was accompanied by a rescue chopper in the event their ship went down. A second team might be carried in the other bird with the two teams to be inserted in different AOs. One or two gunships would escort them and provide fire support if the team ran into trouble upon insertion. A C&C bird with a company officer controlled the insertion, made certain the team was inserted on the correct LZ, and coordinated fire support. The team's radios were tuned to the C&C chopper's frequency. Radio antennas were bent down to prevent rotor strikes.

Small, inconspicuous LZs were selected far enough from suspected enemy areas so as not to attract attention, preferably with a terrain feature, such as a ridge, hill mass, or belt of forest, separating the LZ from the enemy area. Often this could not be done, and LZs might be in close proximity to the enemy. As a deception, the insertion and rescue choppers made multiple landings on scattered LZs, dropping the team on one. Another method was for several choppers to fly in a trail, or column, at treetop level, and the insertion chopper landed, dropped the team, and rejoined the rear of the trail as the other choppers continued on.

Insertion

Insertion was the most intense moment of any mission. Each man was lost in his thoughts, but this was where discipline and training paid off. Troops had to focus and be prepared for any eventuality. The crew chief alerted them a few minutes out from the LZ. The TL leaned out the door, straining to confirm it was the right LZ. Landing on the wrong LZ, even a few hundred yards away, would make it extremely difficult to determine the team's actual location in the dense forest with scarce identifiable landmarks. The team's survival and ability to report accurate locations demanded it know its location precisely at all times, and unfortunately it was all too common for pilots to insert on the wrong LZ.

The chopper came in fast, flared, and went into ground effect a few feet off the red dirt. The team might all go out the same side and rush into the trees without slowing. Alternatively, they could also go out both doors, hit the ground, and move out once the chopper departed. This took only seconds. If they were fired upon they knew not to fire from within the helicopter for danger of hitting the chopper, a crewman, or their own men. If only one man was out the door and fire was received they all exited. It was a dash to the nearest concealment, and they halted after 330–1,000ft (100–300m) in a tight circle, kneeling, alert, and weapons ready. After the chopper departed it was startlingly quiet, and the team listened for sounds of movement and signal shots, and accustomed themselves to the natural sounds. The TL had the radio handset to his ear. Once assured they were safe he gave an all-clear to the C&C bird and a commo check was made with the other radio. The C&C and gunships would orbit nearby on standby. Noses were counted and equipment checked to ensure nothing was dropped. Satisfied, the TL reported his direction of movement and then moved out in a file formation.

The most experienced scout was the pointman with his weapon set on full automatic. The TL followed with the radio operators behind him, then a scout. The assistant patrol leader brought up the rear as the "tail gunner." A wedge or diamond formation might be used in sparse vegetation, but the file was faster (when necessary), quieter, easier to control, and less tiring in dense vegetation as only one trail was busted. It created a less detectable trail than an extended formation, which made a wider path. The interval depended on vegetation, but it was typically close. Each man was assigned a sector of observation and he carried his weapon ready, moving with his eyes. Troops were alert for any unnatural sounds or disruption of normal sounds, the least flicker of movement, and anything that appeared out of place or man-made.

Their pace was deliberate and painstakingly slow. Each toe-heel step was made with caution, the toe feeling for twigs, crackling dead leaves, and loose rocks before

BELOW
A LRP team is inserted by a Huey using flexible aluminum ladders. These ladders have only 12in-wide rungs as opposed to the more common 36in rungs. The latter ladder had a propensity of whipping around in the rotor-wash. (US Army)

BELOW BOTTOM
LRPs cling to the extraction ladder at a couple of thousand feet above ground level. They have clipped themselves on with snap links. The ladder could also be used to insert a team from a hovering chopper. There were instances when troops were dragged through treetops as choppers avoided fire. (US Army)

A LRP team moves through shoulder-high elephant grass. This was the typical height, but it could reach as high as 8ft, restricting a man's field of observation to arm's length. (John Burford collection)

firmly planting the heel. Movement was painfully slow, sometimes with only a couple of hundred yards covered per hour. They followed the terrain contour, keeping to the most densely vegetated areas and zigzagging through the AO. Map corrections, water points, LZs, and trails were marked. Arm and hand signals were used to relay actions and warnings. When it was necessary to speak, the message was whispered into an ear and relayed man to man.

 RAPPELLING

Rappelling from a UH-1D Huey was used to insert teams when LZs were unavailable, or to simply avoid using the few LZs in an area as they might be under surveillance. It was a less-than-desirable means of insertion as it required special rigging of the helicopter, preparatory training for the team, and exposed the helicopter in a hover at between 50ft and over 100ft for several minutes. Only four rappelling ropes could be rigged. With four heavily loaded LRPs, a rappelmaster, and the four-man crew, it would require a second chopper to insert the rest of the team. Rappelling is relatively safe although the rucksack and weapons made it cumbersome. Web gear could not be worn and had to be secured to the rucksack. The only equipment needed by the individual was a 12ft sling rope to form a rappel seat, heavy duty work gloves, and a snap link. The 120ft 5/8in diameter nylon ropes were dropped either coiled around a log, 16-24in long and 2-3in in diameter, or a sandbag to carry the rope to the ground. The rappelmaster ordered the men to hook up, checked for proper attachment, assisted them out the door as they stood on the skips, and gave the order to rappel. If a rope tangled in vegetation the rappelmaster would cut it. The ropes were designed to stretch and a log book was kept on each. Once they had stretched to 140ft or showed excessive wear they were replaced.

A 2qt bladder-type canteen, one of several models. Note the Velcro-closed water purification tablet bottle pocket on the case. Depending on the season and area, water shortages could be a serious problem for LRPs. (Trey Moore collection)

SALUTE report

The SALUTE report format was used to ensure the following information was accurate and complete:

Size of enemy force
Activities of the enemy force, including general direction of movements
Location given by six- or eight-digit coordinates
Unit identification of enemy including markings, symbols, and uniforms
Time and date of sighting using 24-hour military time system; equipment carried by the enemy including weapons, web gear, and vehicles

Extra precautions were used to cross danger areas. Efforts were taken to prevent scuffing the sides of stream banks and gullies, while roads and trails might be crossed in single file with each man stepping in the footprints of the others to minimize tracks and to prevent the team's strength from being determined. Another technique was for the team to position themselves along the trail and to all cross at once, minimizing their exposure and preventing the team from being split if engaged. The first individuals crossing a gully or other rough terrain learned to slow their pace to allow the following men time to get across and not become separated. Unless a reconnaissance objective, villages and cultivated areas were avoided and bypassed downwind. Crossing a stream meant a short halt to fill canteens, with halazone purification tablets added at the next break.

It was difficult for many commanders to comprehend the slow movement rate necessary for LRPs to remain undetected. They could not always understand the limitations of the team's visibility at ground level in the jungle or that from atop a jungle-covered hill they could see nothing but trees.

Radios were normally turned off to conserve batteries. Batteries burned up quickly and only a limited number of 4.12lb (1.9kg) "bats" could be carried. Radios were only turned on if it appeared enemy contact was imminent. Required contacts were made at specified times three or four times a day to report the team's location, movement direction, and status. In AOs out of radio range a helicopter would overfly the area several times a day to make contact. When reporting enemy activity a SALUTE report was made (see sidebar).

Grid coordinates were transmitted by a "shackle code." This was a simple low-level code for encrypting grid coordinates. It consisted of a predetermined ten-letter word with no two letters the same; BLACKNIGHT for example. It was a simple substitution code with the letters assigned 1–0. When transmitting a six-digit coordinate the radio operator would say, "I shackle, Charlie, November, Kilo, Bravo, Alpha, Lima. How copy? Over." Using BLACKNIGHT as the code word, the base station would repeat the phonetic letters; in this case standing for "465132." Another means was a "KAC code," a pocket-sized "wiz-wheel" for converting numbers to letters.

Many missions were a so-called "dry hole" with nothing found. This was of value as it was important to know where the enemy were not located or whether they had moved out of an area. Patrols might also find indications of the size of the force that had occupied a base camp and in what direction it departed. It was common for a team to be extracted from such an AO in a day or so or even hours; sometimes to be reinserted in a nearby AO.

A team would move until dusk, with just enough light remaining to see by. The leader would select a "remain overnight" (RON) position, discretely point it out, and continue past. The team hooked back to the designated RON and immediately took up position covering their backtrail in case they were being followed. A RON was often compared to a miniskirt: it offered minimal cover and concealment, all-around security, and can be defended for a short time. LRPs might move a short distance after darkness fell to further deceive the enemy. The RON was within dense vegetation well away from trails, streams, lines of drift, and easily traversed terrain. Claymores were emplaced on avenues of approach. The team might assume a "wagon-wheel" formation in the prone, facing outward with their feet in the center. This allowed them to alert one another by tapping boots. An alternative was to sit back-to-back in a tight circle resting on their rucksacks. At rest, weapons and equipment were checked and cleaned without disassembly, and a radio report was made. Troops slept in that position without a bedroll. If the enemy was about, even when it rained, LRPs did not use ponchos as they made noise and glistened. To further minimize the chances of discovery insect repellent was relied upon rather than mosquito nets. Everything was kept packed and ready to move out with only necessary items removed from the ruck. Troops did not shave or brush their teeth, and they removed one boot at a time when checking their feet.

Seldom was a situation such that meals could be heated. Issue heat tablets or burning balls of C4 and food odors were too conspicuous. LRP or C-rations were usually eaten cold, and in the case of LRPs, dry. On longer missions, especially in the rains, hot meals were prepared well away from possible enemy areas, while tepid drinking water was flavored with presweetened Kool-Aid® sent from home.

Night movement was avoided. It made too much noise, was too slow, and there was too much of a chance of running into an enemy camp or ambush. There were no night vision goggles at the time – and there is nothing darker than a jungle floor at night. Moving on trails was suicide.

Contact

The following describes a typical example of what would happen when an LRP team encountered the enemy.

The team is awake and alert as dawn approaches. They quickly eat, and when it is light enough, they move out, recovering the Claymores. They soon find a yard-wide trail one-third of the way up a ridge with recent footprints leaving telltale tire tread marks. They parallel the trail, moving a few paces at a time: halting, listening, moving, but never setting foot on the trail itself. The team discovers a site where a fallen tree branch has recently been cut to clear the trail. At another point where streamlets trickle out of the ridge side, new bamboo mats have been laid over the muddy trail. The team plots the trail's coordinates and continue on.

A chance contact, the accidental meeting with an enemy patrol or even individuals on routine duties in a base area, were the most common contacts. Once a team was discovered it was "compromised." With the enemy aware of its presence, the LRP team could no longer accomplish its mission. The enemy quickly learned how dangerous a LRP team was with their ability to call in artillery, air strikes, and gunships, let alone report his activities. Every effort would be made to destroy a LRP team, with even rear service troops turning out to sweep the area. It did not require highly trained troops to keep the LRPs on the run, and if discovering them, to fix them so that they could be destroyed. For the LRPs, keen alertness was essential, not just to avoid ambushes, but to ensure it was they who detected the enemy first. This guaranteed a distinct advantage in a close-range firefight.

The trail leads downward and crosses the stream at the bottom of the ridge and then climbs up the opposite ridge. The team backs off and cautiously crosses further downstream. Angling up the side of the jungle-covered ridge now above the trail, the pointman sees a flicker of movement and signals "hasty ambush left." The men ease into prone positions. Most are not certain from exactly which angle the threat approaches due to the ground vegetation blocking their view of each other just a couple of yards away.

ABOVE TOP
An XM177E2 submachine gun-armed LRP team leader, carrying his own radio, signals his men to quickly cross a rice paddy. Sometimes such exposure could not be avoided owing to the size of the paddies. (US Army)

ABOVE
An AN/PRC-25 radio carried on a makeshift shoulder sling. This was sometimes used when occupying an observation post when keeping a trail under surveillance, and the rucksack was left in a patrol base to the rear. (US Army)

The TL is forced to make a quick decision. If it appears the enemy, whom he estimates at at least eight if not more, will pass them, his troops will merely hide. But it will be a different matter if the enemy moves directly toward the team. The LRP hears voices above them. The VC patrol is less than 100ft (30m) away higher up the ridge, heading down toward the team, perhaps to the stream. The VC looking down the slope can see only vegetation, but the team can see brush moving, and then it sees canvas-booted feet.

With signaling impossible, the team is prepared to do whatever the TL initiates. He removes a grenade, rotates the safety clip, and lays it on the ground. He aims his XM177E2 above a pair of boots, partly exhales, and squeezes the trigger shouting, "Fire!" in case his weapon fails. The team's response is immediate, and all weapons blast away with rapid semiautomatic shots.[14] The TL chucks his grenade and reloads. More grenades detonate with crashing bangs. Answering fire is erratic and high, snapping over the brush, an advantage of being positioned downslope. Rattling AK bursts clatter from the right and higher up. High-pitched shouts, bodies thrusting through brush, scrambling feet; a grenade detonates behind the TL, and twigs and leaves shower down. Shrieks emit from the cloud as other team members throw frags.

"Peal to six o'clock," shouts the TL, ordering a disengagement in the direction they had traveled from. The pointman empties his weapon on full-auto, and crouching low, darts past the TL who throws a grenade, empties his magazine, and runs to the rear. Each man sequentially chucks a frag and empties his weapon in a "banana peel," the means of breaking contact while keeping up a continuous barrage of fire and grenades. Finally the assistant TL lobs a CS grenade followed by a frag, and as he departs he drops a white smoke. AK bursts crackle behind them amid shouts. They leave "Charlie" in confusion, but the VC might soon be on their trail. The team closes up, and the assistant TL sends up the count, tapping on the man in front, saying, "One." That man taps the man ahead of him. "Two." When the count comes to the TL, the number five, he knows the pointman is ahead; all men are accounted for. The TL signals a halt, and the men coil into a tight circle to assess casualties. One scout took a deep graze in his side, and it is quickly dressed. A team member shoulders the injured man's ruck. One of the radio operators has two grenade fragments in his thigh and one in the hand, but

14 Full automatic fire wastes ammunition and is inaccurate, even at short ranges.

G **CONTACT**

An extraction under pressure, that is, engaged by a closely pursuing enemy force, was among the most dangerous actions LRPs encountered. All manner of techniques were used to break contact with a pursuing enemy force: minimizing tracks, laying deceptive trails, ambushing the back-trail, deploying trip-wired grenades and Claymores, tear gas and smoke grenades, calling artillery fire on the back-trail, wading down streams, and crossing rocky ground. A combination of these techniques were used, with the goal of giving the enemy an excuse to quit the pursuit. The team being pursued had much more to lose and could use extraordinary measures to outrun the enemy. Attack helicopters were invaluable in suppressing pursuers. Their 7.62mm machine gun and 40mm grenade launcher fire could be brought in extremely close. It was a different matter with their less-accurate 2.75in rockets. Essential to a successful extraction under pressure was for the team to be able to accurately mark its position, so that gunships and extraction choppers could locate them and have a reference point from which to engage the unseen enemy.

neither injury is very serious. As they start moving, both radios are turned on, and the TL sends in the contact report that includes location, time, who initiated contact, range, friendly and enemy casualties, and present situation. He requests immediate extraction, sends the codeword for the nearest PZ, and gives his estimated time of arrival (ETA). Having engaged roughly 12 VC, the team is on the run from a superior force. There is a contingency PZ, Tango Six, down the ridge, but this is two "klicks," or two kilometers (1.2 miles) away. A CS grenade is popped behind them so its cloud will hang around the trees. The team works its way up the ridge staying below the crest, where a shallow gully angles upward.

They file into it, intentionally leaving scuff marks. Halfway up, they rig a trip-wired Claymore across the gully as a "mousetrap." Two men move up to the head of the gully and set up a trip-wired frag with a CS grenade taped on and arm it after the team passes. At the same time they hear a shot from behind and then an answering signal shot from the opposite ridge. The enemy is now closing in from two directions.

The TL calls for artillery fire giving a six-digit coordinate on the opposite ridge. After ten minutes, "Shot. Out." comes over the radio followed shortly by "Splash. Out." Seconds later, six plumes of black smoke blossom on the ridge, followed by dull thumps. "Up two hundred, right one hundred. Over." Six more rounds impact in an effort to slow anyone attempting to cut them off. As they press on there are more enemy signal shots from the opposite ridge. More artillery, or "arty," is called for, and rounds slam into the ridge until a "check fire" is called. The C&C bird and a gunship are inbound as the sharp crack of a Claymore echoes behind them, causing some amusement among team members.

A scout crouches at the edge of the brush flashing a marker panel as the two choppers come into view. The C&C bird acknowledges them and reports the PZ is 650ft (200m) ahead. The TL requests rockets halfway up their ridge, and the accompanying Cobra gunship starts its run between the ridgetops. White lances of smoke slant into the trees with dirty gray explosions. But the VC are still closing in.

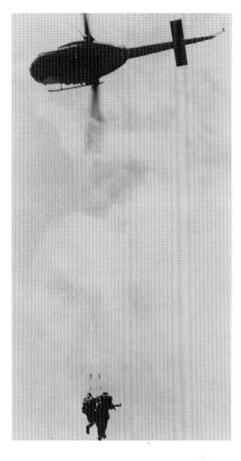

The distinctive whack of Huey blades is heard; the extraction and rescue birds are black dots barreling toward the team below the height of the ridge. The gunship makes another rocket run on the other side of the ridge, preserving a few vital rockets to cover the extraction.

Halting short of the PZ, the scouts move forward to check it out as the TL notifies the C&C they have arrived. As a rule, all choppers monitor the conversation during extractions, but only the C&C talks directly to the TL to prevent confusion. A quick exchange follows. C&C: "Mark your location." TL: "Roger, popping smoke." The TL signals a scout, who tosses a yellow smoke on the PZ's edge. TL: "Identify smoke." C&C: "Lemon." TL: "Roger, lemon." The ground element never told the airborne element what color they were popping as the enemy could monitor the frequency and would attempt to confuse the choppers by popping the same color elsewhere.

A grenade detonates behind them and rifles crackle as two green-clad figures dart over the crest with AKs blazing. The assistant TL throws his last grenade, and all hands fire as the scouts rush back to add their firepower. Warning that the PZ is hot, the TL pops a mini red smoke to mark their precise location, the red indicating danger. The gunship rolls over the crest with a solid stream of red tracers lashing the trees. The TL orders a peelback to the PZ as the assistant TL empties his weapon. Few grenades remain as the extraction bird comes in at full throttle. The assistant and a scout half-drag the wounded radio operator to the bird as it flares and sets down. The remaining frags and white smokes are thrown as inaccurate VC shots

ABOVE
Two LRP are lifted out of a PZ using McGuire rigs. No more than three men could be extracted at a time using this system, and it would require two choppers to take out a five- or six-man team. (John Burford collection)

OPPOSITE PAGE
Among reeds a LRP guides a Huey onto a sandbar for extraction. River-bend sandbars served as PZs when other clearings were unavailable. Note the taped M16A1 muzzle protecting it from water and dust. The tape could be shot through without removing it. (US Army)

RIGHT
LRP team leader John Burford upon returning from a mission. Burford is the author of two books on LRPs. On his belt are magazine pouches, a canteen in the front for easy access, and other canteen carriers holding 20-round magazines. On his right suspender are a strobe light and a serum albumin can and on the left is an M18 smoke grenade. (John Burford collection)

BELOW
Many medical evacuation ("medevac" or "dust-off") helicopters were fitted with a power hoist and a jungle penetrator. Its yellow bullet-like shape and weight allowed it to be lowered through trees by its steel cable. On the ground one of three seats was pulled down, and there was a securing strap for the man to be hoisted. Only one man could be hoisted at a time. (Lone Star Flight Museum)

continue to crackle out of the smoke. Men dive into the bird with the TL the last to fling himself in, after taking a moment to ensure all are aboard. The gunship makes another pass as the bird lifts off with the door gunner hammering rounds into the trees. As it drops down the ridge and flies up the valley, the gunship makes a last pass, expending its rockets.

The blast of cool air gushes through the doors over the gasping men. Grinning in relief, they give each other the thumbs up. As they wing to base, two team members change the radio operator's sodden dressing and the pilot relays the team's condition to the C&C.

As the chopper settles on the pad, uncommitted teams greet the returnees, who soon make their way to the O&I section for debriefing. All aspects of the mission are discussed: insertion to extraction; terrain conditions; map corrections; route; communications problems; fire support; enemy sightings and facilities; enemy uniforms, weapons, equipment, tactics, and activities; and all other aspects of the mission – essentially, what went right and what went wrong.

Debriefing includes the entire team, although individual sessions are also conducted. For critical missions a representative from the headquarters requesting the mission might be present. Debriefing forms are completed and signed by the TL. After a day or two off, they begin planning the next mission.

H

AWARD CEREMONY
LRP/Ranger units were among the most highly decorated units in Vietnam. It required a great deal of skill and valor just to conduct "routine" operations with such a small number of men, deep within enemy territory. The most common decorations for valor were the Silver Star, Bronze Star, and Army Commendation Medal. The latter two were also awarded for service, but when presented for valor, a small bronze "V" device was affixed to the ribbon. The Purple Heart was presented to those wounded in action. These Rangers of Company H, 75th Infantry, attached to the 1st Cavalry Division, wear the traditional black Ranger beret with the 75th Infantry flash, and their unit scroll on the left shoulder in the traditional Ranger colors of red, white, and black. The staff sergeant to the left is Ranger- and airborne-qualified, as is the company commander presenting the decorations, who had served with the 173rd Airborne Brigade in a previous tour, signified by wearing his former combat unit's patch on the right shoulder.

AFTERMATH OF BATTLE

For their frequent actions in which six men opposed twice that number or were pursued by a force potentially in the hundreds, for the casualties they caused by calling in fire, and for the damage they indirectly inflicted on the enemy by their intelligence collection, LRPs were generously presented with many decorations for valor. Three LRP/Rangers received the Medal of Honor, and hundreds of other awards for valor were also bestowed upon them. Between the LRP/Ranger companies/detachments a total of one Presidential Unit Citation, nine Valorous Unit Awards, four Meritorious Unit Commendations, 30 Vietnamese Cross of Gallantry Unit Citations, and 16 Vietnamese Civil Action Medal Unit Citations were granted. About 340 LRPs and Rangers were lost in combat, excluding a few in the early provisional units, for which separate records were not kept. Nine are carried as missing in action.

Regardless of the dangers, stress, and physical strain, a surprising number of LRPs extended their tours up to six months. Some preferred breaking brush as a LRP in Vietnam to monotonous Stateside duty. Many LRPs, after completing their two or three years, simply left the Army. Others reenlisted and went on to serve in the 82nd Airborne Division or the Special Forces, or joined the new Ranger battalions raised in 1974. Only three active Ranger companies remained after 1972; the two Stateside companies (A-75, B-75) were committed to Germany, and one to Alaska (O-75) from 1970 to 1972. They were accompanied by four National Guard companies, reduced to two by 1977. The two companies destined for Germany were deactivated in 1974 to provide manning spaces for the two Ranger battalions. It was not until 1985 that Active Army units, now called long-range surveillance (LRS), began to be activated again.

A LRP team returns from a mission. The man in the center carries a 12-gauge pump shotgun, popular with point men, and a Chinese 7.62mm Type 56 (AK-47) assault rifle. It may have been captured or carried by the point man. (US Army)

The LRPs had their detractors, who felt they drew off too much talented manpower, that their missions were often of too short a duration, that they required too much support when extracted, too frequently required other units to rescue them, or who did not like the elitist attitude displayed by some. Regardless, the LRPs more than adequately proved their value.

While no fewer than 18 memoirs and novels have been published about LRPs, only two movies have touched on the subject. *84 Charlie MoPic*[15] (1989) depicts a cameraman accompanying a LRP team to record lessons learned. The *Odd Angry Shot* (1979) is actually about the Australian SAS conducting LRP missions in Vietnam, but it provides a view of the experiences of a LRP unit.

15 84C was the MOS of a motion picture cameraman.

COLLECTIONS, MUSEUMS, AND RE-ENACTMENT

There is no single museum that highlights the LRPs and Rangers in Vietnam. Examples of uniforms, insignia, and equipment can be found in the Airborne and Special Operations Museum at Fort Bragg, NC, and in the National Infantry Museum at Fort Benning, GA. Items will also be found in the remaining divisional museums of units that served in Vietnam as well as in various private Vietnam War museums. The most extensive collections of LRP/Ranger items are found among private collectors. Collectors are urged to use extreme caution when purchasing items that are reputed to be authentic LRP/Ranger. There are a few LRP/Ranger reenactment groups honoring the memory of these unique units.

For a site detailing individual equipment see: http://www.vietnamgear.com/.

The 75th Ranger Regiment Association: http://www.75thrra.com/.

BIBLIOGRAPHY

Burford, John, *LRRPs in Action*, Squadron/Signal Publications, Carrolton, TX (1985)
—— *LRRP Team Leader*, Ballantine Books, NY (1994)
Camper, Frank, *L.R.R.P.: The Professional*, Dell Publishing, NY (1988)
Chambers, Larry, *Death in the A Shau Valley: L Company LRRPs in Vietnam, 1969–1970*, Ivy Books, NY (1998)
Ebert, James R., *A Life in a Year: The American Infantryman in Vietnam 1965–1972*, Ballantine Books, NY (1993)
Field, Ron, *Ranger: Behind the Lines in Vietnam*, Publishing News, London (2000)
Gebhardt, James F., *Eyes Behind the Lines: US Army Long-Range Reconnaissance and Surveillance Units*, Combat Studies Institute Press, Fort Leavenworth, KS (2005). Online at: http://www-cgsc.army.mil/carl/download/csipubs/gebhardt_LRRP.pdf.
Jorgenson, Kregg P. J., *LRRP Company Command: The Cav's LRP/Rangers in Vietnam, 1968–1969*, Ballantine Books, NY (2000)
—— *The Ghosts of the Highlands: The 1st Cav LRRPs in Vietnam, 1966–67*, Ivy Books, NY (1999)
Lanning, Michael Lee, *Inside the LRRPs: Rangers in Vietnam*, Ivy Books, NY (1988)
Linderer, Gary A., *Eyes Behind the Lines: L Company Rangers in Vietnam, 1969*, Presidio Press, Novato, CA (1991)
—— *Phantom Warriors: LRRPs, LRPs, and Rangers in Vietnam*, Ballantine Books, NY (2001)
—— *Six Silent Men: 101st LRP/Rangers*, Ballantine Books, NY (1996)
—— *The Eyes of the Eagle: F Company LRPs in Vietnam, 1968*, Ballantine Books, NY (1991)
Lyles, Kevin., *Vietnam: US Uniforms in Colour Photographs*, Europa Militaria Special No. 3, Windrow & Greene, London (1992)
Miraldi, Paul W., *Uniforms and Equipment of US Army LRRPs and Rangers in Vietnam 1965–1971*, Schiffer Publishing, Atglen, PA (1999)
Shanahan, Bill, and John P. Brackin., *Stealth Patrol: The Making of a Vietnam Ranger*, Da Capo Press, Cambridge, MA (2003)
Stanton, Shelby L., *Rangers in Vietnam: Combat Recon in Vietnam*, Orion Books, NY (1992)
—— *US Army Uniforms in the Vietnam War*, Stackpole Books, Harrisburg, PA (1992)
US Army, *Infantry Long-Range Patrol Company*, FM 31–18, January 1965.
—— *Long-Range Reconnaissance Patrol Company*, FM 31–18, August 1968.

INDEX